Simple

SEWING

with Lola Nova

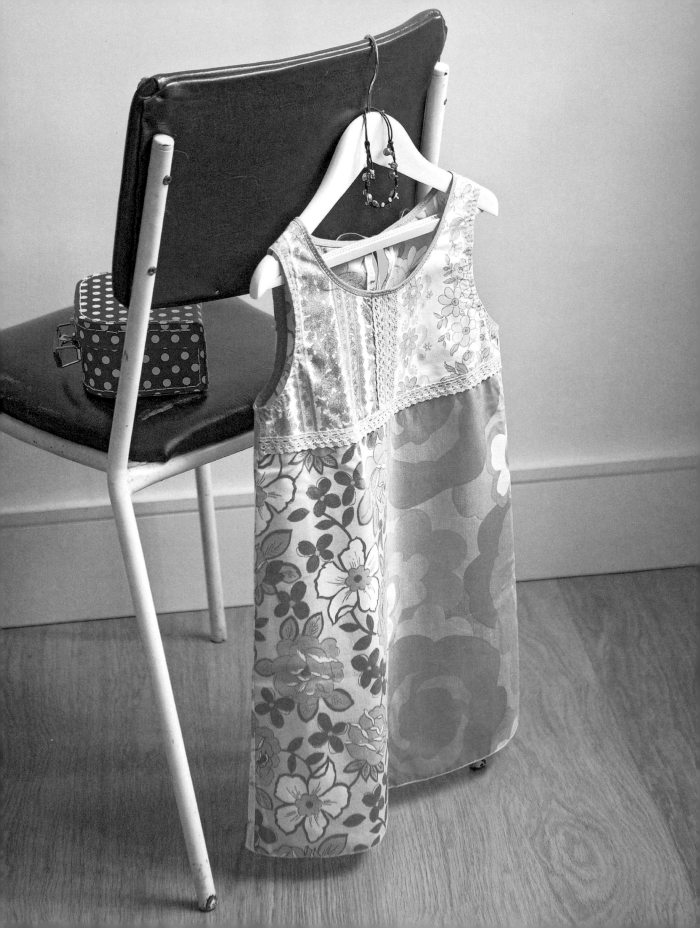

Creative Makers

Simple
SEWING
with Lola Nova

With 25 stylish step-by-step projects that celebrate your handmade life

ALEXANDRA SMITH

PHOTOGRAPHY BY YUKI SUGIURA • DESIGNED BY ANITA MANGAN

Mitchell Beazley

Simple Sewing with Lola Nova

First published in Great Britain in 2012 by Mitchell Beazley,
an imprint of Octopus Publishing Group Ltd,
Endeavour House, 189 Shaftesbury Avenue,
London WC2H 8JY
www.octopusbooks.co.uk

An Hachette UK Company
www.hachette.co.uk

ISBN 978 1 84533 698 1

A CIP record for this book is available from the British Library.

Set in Berthold Akzidenz Grotesk and Bulmer.

Printed and bound in China.

Publisher – Alison Starling
Senior Art Editor – Juliette Norsworthy
Designer – Anita Mangan
Assistant Designer – Abi Read
Senior Editor – Leanne Bryan
Copy Editor – Katie Hardwicke
Proofreader – Emma Clegg
Indexer – Helen Snaith
Senior Production Controller – Lucy Carter
Photographer – Yuki Sugiura
Stylist – Cynthia Inions

Key to project level

 easy   intermediate   difficult

Introduction 6 • Tools for Your Sewing Kit 8 • Fabric, Trims, Buttons, Bits & Bobs 10 • Fabric-painting 12 • Attaching Bias Binding 14 • Very Simple Pattern-drafting & Modification 16 • Finishing Touches 20

THE PROJECTS

Templates 132 • Glossary 140 • Resources 141 • Index 142 • Acknowledgements 144

INTRODUCTION

Lola Nova began in a small lavender bedroom inside the Little Green Cottage. There was a baby on the way: there were curtains to sew; cosy quilts to make; cloth nappies with tricky gussets to stitch; and tiny outfits to fashion. There was much to do and not much money to work with. A pretty bed sheet from the linen closet became a curtain, scraps from my grandmother's fabric bin were turned into a quilt, flannel shirts were cut into soft cloth nappies, and outfits were made from this and that (I recall a wee pair of crazy looking trousers made from an old tablecloth!).

As I stitched away in a state of fevered nesting, it occurred to me that I loved every minute of it, every stitch: every new challenge became a tiny revelation. I kept pushing myself, stitching over hurdles and frustrations, honing my craft, and experimenting with new techniques and materials. As my skills grew, so did my passion.

As I slowly emerged from my "new mama" bubble a couple of years later, I began reading crafty blogs – and that rich and wild world of like-minded souls drew me in. Since I liked to write, and I liked to craft, I thought I'd take a leap into the unknown. The blog, *Lola Nova – Whatever Lola Wants*, was launched and my creative world blossomed. The support and kindness of a vibrant community of inspiring individuals led me to surprising places. It reunited me with my old flame, photography, inspired the crochet affair, and taught me to see the creative world through fresh eyes. The people I meet, the friends I have made, and the inspiration I have gleaned have been astounding.

My imagination and my passion drive me to create. A piece of me goes into everything I make and I wouldn't have it any other way. Handmade to me is about storytelling,

making connections, sharing a journey and creating something that has heart and soul.

ABOUT THIS BOOK

This book is a labour of love meant to celebrate the handmade life. Use materials you love, to create what you love for your home, family and friends. My hope is to inspire the passionate crafter in you to give new life to treasured pieces, to re-imagine and repurpose while trying new techniques, materials and ideas for a modern life.

I have arranged the book into chapters based on Boho, Natural, Vintage, Eclectic and Whimsy style. Each contains projects inspired by these themes. Step-by-step instructions guide the beginner through simple projects while providing inspiration and challenges for the more advanced seamstress or tailor.

Embrace your craft, learn old tricks while trying something new, and remember that we all make mistakes along the way. In my making life, I have never made a mistake and not learned something valuable from it. Be bold, play, take risks and, most of all, have fun!

Happy sewing!

TOOLS FOR YOUR SEWING KIT

To complete the projects in this book, you will need just a few basics in your sewing kit, along with a couple of extra pieces of equipment for specific jobs. Start with what is most essential and build up the rest of your kit along the way.

The essentials

✿ **Sewing machine** A good quality sewing machine is a must. It should have the basic stitches (straight stitch in different stitch lengths), a couple of zigzag stitch options, the capability to sew buttonholes and a strong motor to pierce through heavyweight fabrics. A zipper foot and decorative stitch options would be a bonus.

✿ **Iron and ironing board** Keeping your fabric smooth and wrinkle-free and pressing seams and hems as you work will help to ensure straight lines and matching seams.

✿ **Cutting tools** There are three basic types of scissors that are an absolute necessity: a sharp pair of fabric scissors – only use them for fabric and thread as paper or other materials will dull them quickly; small sharp scissors, like embroidery scissors, are perfect for cutting threads, clipping seams, and precision cutting; and household scissors for cutting paper, elastic and anything other than fabric. You should also have a seam ripper.

✿ **Needles, pins and pincushions** Your sewing kit should have a good supply of needles in a variety of sizes both for hand sewing and embroidery.

✿ **Sewing machine needles** for different types of fabric are essential. Change your needles often – roughly after every 12 hours of sewing.

✿ **Straight pins** are indispensable for marking, pinning and attaching. Look for long sharp steel pins with glass heads (they won't melt under an iron). Keep your pins tidy in a pincushion.

✿ **Safety pins** have a myriad of uses, from threading elastic through casing to holding and attaching fabric.

✿ **Thread** Always use good quality, new sewing thread to match or contrast with your project. Keep embroidery thread in several colours in your kit, ready for when you need to add a hand-embroidered embellishment for a finishing touch.

✿ **Measuring tools** Use a sturdy flexible tape measure for taking measurements and marking out fabric pieces. A long ruler, preferably a clear acrylic quilter's type, provides a solid line to measure and mark against, and the extra length makes measuring longer patterns much simpler than using a standard ruler. Keep a smaller, standard ruler for tight spaces.

✿ **Marking tools** For marking seams, centre points, necklines, templates and reference points use a fabric-marker pen or pencil. Air- or water-soluble markers leave a semi-permanent mark. Tailor's chalk is ideal for use on dark fabrics. Have a selection of pencils, pens and coloured pencils to hand for making notes and drawing up plans or patterns.

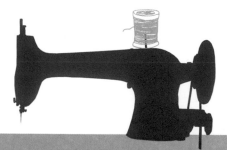

Fabric-painting kit

You will need a few pieces of special equipment, along with a pencil, fabric, craft knife and self-healing mat.

✪ **Fabric paint** Used for stencilling. It often needs to be heat set with an iron before it can be washed but read the manufacturer's instructions in advance as not all fabric paints have the same requirements. Use a palette or plastic container to hold your paint (something you don't mind getting stained).

✪ **Freezer paper** Used for creating stencils. It is backed with a shiny plastic coating that will stick to fabric when pressed with an iron, but which peels off easily. You draw or trace designs onto the paper side of the freezer paper, cut out a stencil and then use fabric paint to put your design on the fabric surface of your project.

✪ **Foam craft brush** Used to apply the fabric paint in combination with a stencil or rubber stamp. I find a 2.5cm (1in) size to be the most useful. Clean your brushes after use with water, then let them air dry.

✪ **Rubber stamps** You can also apply fabric paint with craft rubber stamps. Always wash your stamps with water after use and let them air dry.

Extras – the useful and the super cool

✪ **Fusible interfacing or stabilizer** Used to add structure, body or strength to fabric. It has a coating on one side that fuses to fabric with the heat of an iron. It comes in different weights; light, medium and heavy – I keep a couple of metres of each to hand.

✪ **Paper pattern** Tracing paper, brown craft paper, newsprint and/or printer paper all come in useful. Tracing transfer paper, or dressmakers' carbon paper, is used for transferring markings from patterns onto fabric, tracing embroidery designs and the like.

✪ **Rotary cutter, craft knife, non-slip ruler, and self-healing cutting mat** A rotary cutter is great for cutting through a few layers of fabric at a time, and perfect for achieving long straight lines and accurate cuts when used with a non-slip quilter's ruler. Use a craft knife for precision cutting of stencils. A self-healing mat will protect your work surface when using a rotary cutter or craft knife.

✪ **Pinking shears** These have serrated blades that cut a saw-tooth edge. They can be used to finish a seam on fabrics that do not fray easily, and are great for use on felt and fleece.

✪ **Seam gauge** A small metal ruler with a sliding guide. It is helpful in determining a seam allowance, marking a hem, and various other tasks.

✪ **Bodkin** A great tool for threading elastic through casings, where you feed it in one end of the channel and push it through to emerge at the other end.

✪ **Notebooks** I always keep a notebook handy. I write out plans, sketch up design ideas, keep track of measurements, list the supplies I need, and so on. I also use my notebooks to keep swatches of fabric and pictures for inspiration.

✪ **Organizer** Whether it be a sewing basket, an art caddy, or a repurposed suitcase, have a special place to keep your sewing things organized. I have a few such organizational items; the one I find most useful is a multi-tiered tool box that I got from a hardware store.

FABRIC, TRIMS, BUTTONS, BITS & BOBS

Fabric

Choosing fabric is a truly personal process; some of us are drawn to bold and bright, while others lean towards subdued hues. Whatever you prefer, you want to make sure that the fabric is suitable for your project. Most of the projects in this book call for cotton, linen or other woven fabrics (non-knit fabrics). If you are sewing a project that is going to be getting everyday use, you will want to choose fabrics that can easily be washed, dried and are colourfast. For myself, I prefer natural-fibre fabrics more often than not for their ease of sewing and care. Heavier weight fabrics, such as home-furnishing fabrics, canvas, denim and corduroy, may add more structure and durability to a project that gets a lot of use. Delicate fabrics, such as silks and some vintage fabrics, may be better suited to projects that do not receive constant use or handling. With all that said, it is important to experiment and use what you love so that you love what you make!

New fabric

When buying new fabric, the adage "you get what you pay for" is particularly true. Buy the best you can afford – the results will be much more satisfying. That's not to say there isn't a place for those bargain fabrics, but if you are putting a lot of time and effort into a special quality project, the fabric should be quality too.

I'd like to give you some great advice about what fabrics you should stock up on, what ratio of print to solids you should aim for, but the truth is I don't purchase my fabric that way. I go with my gut or my heart. If it is a fabric that I think I want to use to make a garment, I will purchase 2–3 metres (6½–10 feet). If it is a fabric I absolutely love, but don't know what I might use it for yet, I will purchase ½–1 metre (20 inches – 3 feet). If it's on sale… well, that could go any which way at all!

I don't always have a purpose in mind for the fabric I purchase, sometimes it stays on the shelf for a long time looking pretty, waiting for the day when it jumps out at me "telling" me the story of what it's meant to be. Purchasing fabric that really "speaks" to me helps to shape my decision making in the fabric store; it keeps me from buying fabric that I think "might do in a pinch" and curbs my hoarding tendencies. The moral of this story is: buy what you love! Oh, and throw in a solid, dot, stripe or check every once in a while.

I'll admit to being one of those people that wash and dry my fabric right after I bring it home (to allow for any shrinkage). I have been frustrated too many times in wanting to use a fabric for a project "right this minute" then realizing I need to wait for a wash and dry. Information on the proper care of particular fabrics can often be found on the end of the fabric bolt in the shop.

TIP: LINING FABRICS

For the projects in this book, it is important to choose lining fabrics that have the same care requirements as the main project fabric, for ease of use and peace of mind.

Vintage and formerly loved fabrics

My collection of vintage linens started early, thanks to my grandmother and my mother. A few pieces raided from their linen closets long ago, has turned into a lifelong treasure hunt. I pick up my vintage pieces from many sources: charity shops, garage sales, car boot sales and online sellers. I have even coerced my mother to be on the lookout for me. Vintage sheets, tablecloths, curtains, napkins, tea towels, doilies and suchlike. often make their way into my designs.

Another source of formerly loved fabrics comes from second-hand clothing. Sometimes I come across a piece of clothing that I would never wear personally, but the fabric is fantastic. I take it home, give it a good wash and press, then cut it apart along the seams. You can get a considerable amount of fabric from a full skirt, long dress or large men's shirt. These pieces are also a great source of buttons.

TIP: VINTAGE FABRIC CARE

I wash all of my vintage fabric and linens before use. After years of exposure to vintage textiles, I can usually determine if I can put something in the wash or if it needs a handwash or simple soak. If you have any doubts, handwash vintage textiles in cold water with a mild washing-up liquid. Anything vintage with bright colours should be washed separately, as the dyes used may not be colourfast. It is generally a good idea to air dry most vintage textiles.

A note on vintage fabrics: Be cautious when using vintage fabrics on items for use by children. Some heavy metals, such as lead, were used in fabric dyes and especially on screen-printed designs. If you have any doubts, it's best to pass and use something else.

Bits & bobs

I like to keep a good selection of trims and buttons to hand, so I pick them up from many different sources. I find it good to keep a variety of plain-coloured ribbons and ricrac in my stash along with vintage lace, novelty ribbons, and the like. Look out for a bargain sale at your local sewing store to stock up on ribbons and trims.

Sometimes you can get lucky and find a treasure box of buttons in a charity shop. Ask your granny, great aunt or a neighbour if they have any they are willing to part with.

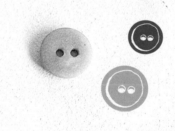

Printing and painting on fabric is one of my favourite techniques, so much so that it has become one of my signature design elements and I have featured it in many of the projects. It is an amazing way to turn something "rather nice" into something "truly awesome"!

Getting started

You will find several stencil designs in the Templates section (see pages 132–9), each corresponding to a project. You can use them as they are, or enlarge them, shrink them, and use them in other projects. There are many other images available for personal use, but always check copyright laws if you intend to reproduce or sell your creations. Another way to print on fabric is by using rubber stamps; this technique is very quick and easy.

Many fabrics are suitable for fabric painting: cottons, linens, T-shirt fabric or jersey, and so on. The fabrics should be heat safe for the iron or dryer for setting most fabric paints. Fabrics with a lot of texture, such as fleece, felts, bouclé, knits, and so on are less desirable. Always test a swatch of your fabric with the fabric paint before moving on to your main project, to make sure it will produce the effect you are after.

Using rubber stamps

1. Apply the paint
Using fabric paint with a foam brush, transfer some paint onto the rubber stamp. **(a)**

2. Print the design
Press the stamp onto the fabric with even, steady pressure and lift away. Repeat the stamp in a pattern to create a custom print fabric. Let the paint dry and set following the fabric paint manufacturer's instructions.

3. Other printing ideas
Look around and see what else you can use as a stamping design. I found a stray lid to a child's marker and a pencil eraser and combined them to make a geometric design. Your options are limitless – now go and have some fun! **(b)**

a

b

Using freezer-paper stencils

1. Trace your design

Decide on an image that you want to use as your stencil and what fabric you are going to stencil on. Cut two pieces of freezer paper a little larger than the image itself. Trace or draw your image onto the paper (dull) side of one piece of freezer paper with a pencil. You will use the second piece later.

2. Cut out the design

Use a craft knife or small scissors to cut out the design. When using a craft knife, be sure to place a self-healing mat underneath to protect your work surface. Begin cutting along the lines of your image – don't cut across from the edge, you need to keep the paper intact. Work slowly and carefully, especially in corners and tight curves. **(c)**

3. Iron the stencil

Place the stencil so that the plastic (shiny) side is facing the fabric. Use a dry iron on a medium setting to press it lightly in place. Now turn the fabric and stencil over and place the second piece of freezer-paper over the back area of the stencil and press in place. This helps to minimize any "bleeding" of the paint and stops the paint coming through onto your work surface. Turn the fabric back over to the stencil side, using the iron to press again to ensure all the edges of your stencil have adhered to the fabric.

4. Paint the design

Before you begin painting, be sure to read the instructions for your brand of fabric paint. Pour some paint into a palette or plastic container and saturate the tip of the foam brush with the paint, wiping away any excess. Begin brushing on the paint from the outer edges of your stencil towards the centre. **(d)**

Continue working from the outer edges in, adding paint to your brush as necessary. Cover the entire stencil area with an even coat of fabric paint. Light-coloured paints, or paint on dark fabrics, may require more than one coat. Let the first coat dry for a couple of hours before applying a second coat. Set the piece aside to dry completely, leaving it overnight usually does the trick. Once the stencil is dry, remove the stencil paper and the backing paper.

5. Set the paint

Follow the manufacturer's instructions. Many fabric paints are heat set. Simply use your iron on the highest heat setting for the fabric you are using, cover the stencil with a pressing cloth, and iron the design for 30 seconds to a minute. Then repeat for the reverse of the fabric.

I am often asked about bias binding; people want me to tell them the secret to applying it. Well, there is no secret. Like many things in life, a perfectly applied bias binding takes practice. I am going to show you a couple of ways to sew on bias binding; the proper method for applying bias binding as a facing, and the quick (cheat's) method to apply it to a hem or edge.

Bias binding

A narrow strip of fabric cut on the bias or cross-grain, bias binding gives the fabric a little bit of stretch or ease, making it perfect for curves and corners.

Bias binding comes in two types and a variety of widths: single fold is flat, with each raw edge folded in towards the centre, wrong sides together. This is the type I use for armhole and neckline facing. It can also be used as a decorative trim. Double fold is single-fold tape that has been folded in half with the single folds to the inside. I use this for binding raw edges, hems and quilts.

Applying bias binding to hems (cheat's method)

This method uses double-fold bias binding and works very well for binding hems, the raw edges of items like bibs, pot holders and some quilts, and is the method used in the Badges & Patches project (see page 120).

1. Attach to a straight edge (hem)

Sandwich the raw edge of your project in between the fold of bias tape and pin in place. If you are working with packaged bias binding, place the wider side of the tape on the wrong side or back of your project.

Stitch the bias binding from the right side of your project close to the folded edge. You may find that using a zigzag or blanket stitch (see Glossary, page 140) works nicely, especially if you are using a narrow bias tape. Remove your pins as you sew. **(a)**

2. Attach to a curve

Press your bias tape to a curve. Fold under one end by approx. 1cm (3/8in). Start by sandwiching the raw edge of the project in between the folds of the tape and start pinning the end with the raw edge to the curve. Ease around the curve, pinning as you go, and overlap the folded end at the starting point. **(b)**

Stitch the bias binding from the right side of your project close to the folded edge.

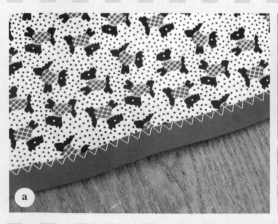

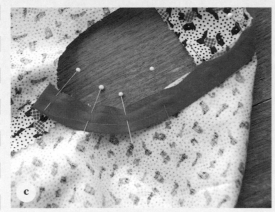

Applying bias binding as facing (proper method)

This method is used for armhole and neckline facing, and uses single-fold bias tape. I recommend trimming your seam to, or using a seam allowance of, 6mm (¼in).

1. Press the binding

Cut the length of bias binding you need for the facing. You can roughly gauge this by draping the bias binding around the opening and then adding a little extra; you can trim this later.

Gently press the length of bias binding into a curve, making sure the curve is in the same direction as the curve on your garment opening.

Open up the bias tape and press under approximately 1cm (³⁄₈in) of one end, wrong sides facing.

2. Pin the binding

If you want the bias to show on the right side of the garment as a design detail, pin your bias binding to the wrong side of the garment.

Open up the bias tape and start with the end of the tape that you have folded under; begin pinning the right side of the bias tape to the wrong side of the garment with the raw edges matching. I like to begin at the underarm seam, or the back centre of the neckline, for a cleaner look. Do not pull or stretch the bias tape as you pin, simply ease the bias tape gently to the curve of your opening. **(c)**

Continue pinning the tape around the entire edge of your opening; overlap the ends by approx. 13mm (½in). Trim off any excess.

3. Sew the binding

Stitch along the folded crease of the bias binding approx. 6mm (¼in) from the edge, removing the pins just before your needle reaches them. Stitch around the entire opening.

4. Finish the right side

Fold the entire width of the bias tape to the right side of your garment, press neatly and pin in place. Stitch the tape close to the folded edge, approx. 3mm (¹⁄₈in), removing the pins as you sew. When you are finished, give it another gentle press. **(d)**

If you do not want the bias tape to show on the outside of your garment, the same process applies; you simply begin by attaching the bias tape to the right side of your garment.

Hooray for bias binding!

For the purposes of this book, I am going to show a couple of rudimentary pattern-making techniques so that you can give it a whirl. The Little Joy Dress (see page 68) uses the techniques outlined here. As a pattern is not included, this is a great opportunity to learn how to replicate a favourite dress, and then modify it. Alternatively you can use a simple commercial A-line pattern with modifications. This will give the block-pieced vintage effect of the Little Joy Dress project. These instructions are suitable for ages 1–5 years, but can easily be adapted for older children or adult sizes. When you draft or modify a pattern I recommend "making a muslin" first. This means creating a test garment from inexpensive material to check for fit, so that you can make any necessary adjustments before cutting and sewing up your special fabric.

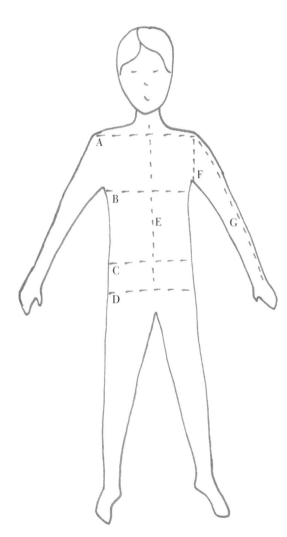

Taking key measurements

Whenever you make a garment, it is always important to have a few key measurements to work from. For the purpose of the projects in this book, we will address just a few of these.

Begin with your child dressed in her underwear or snug-fitting T-shirt and tights. If your little one is still in nappies, measure her with the nappy on. Take the following measurements and record them on a sheet of paper, index card, notebook or similar.

A: Shoulder width Measure across the back at the nape of the neck from shoulder to shoulder.

B: Chest Measure around the fullest part of the chest, under the arms.

C: Waist Measure around the natural waistline just above the navel.

D: Hips Measure around the fullest part of the hips and buttocks.

E: Back neck to waist/hip Measure from the back nape of the neck to the waist and/or hip.

F: Armhole depth/drop Measure from the top outside edge of the shoulder down to the armpit, bring the measuring tape under the armpit and back around up to the shoulder.

G: Sleeve length Have your child extend her arm just out to the side of her body. Measure from the shoulder to the wrist.

Creating a pattern from an existing A-line dress or pinafore

1. Trace an existing garment

Begin by laying out your pattern paper on a large work surface. Lay an existing dress on top of the paper face up (press the garment flat beforehand). Carefully trace around the outside edges of the garment with a dark pencil. **(a)**

Once you have traced the garment, remove it and set it aside. You now have a basic pattern template to start with. Measure across your template in the key areas, to ensure that what you have drawn will fit your child comfortably.

2. Copy the template

This first template is the back pattern template. Now make an exact copy of this template for the front pattern template. Either lay the garment on fresh paper and trace around it again, or trace your first template.

Your garment will most likely have a deeper neckline in the front, as well as a slightly deeper armhole. If you are not comfortable drawing it freehand, lay your garment inside the traced outline, put a piece of carbon tracing transfer paper under the garment at the neckline and armholes with the coloured side facing the pattern paper. Using a blunt utensil, rub along the edge of the front neckline and armholes. This will transfer your markings for the placement of the front neckline and armhole.

Draw over the markings with your pencil to complete the basic front template.

3. Add seam allowances

I generally use a 1cm (³⁄₈in) seam allowance, but a 1.5cm (⁵⁄₈in) allowance is also standard. Use what you are comfortable with, but be consistent. Using a seam gauge or ruler, begin measuring and marking out from the side seams of your template. I use a dashed line for speed, then draw over it. **(b)**

I use a narrower seam allowance at the neckline and armhole to accommodate the bias tape facing, here I've added a 6mm (¼in) seam allowance for 13mm (½in) bias tape. For the bottom hem, I added a 2.5cm (1in) allowance. Make a note of all the seam allowances, measurements and pattern size, and mark "Front" and "Back" directly onto the relevant pattern templates as you work.

4. Cut out the pattern

Now you need to fold the paper in half along the centre line of the template. To find the centre, measure across the width of the outline of the dress at the bottom, waist and neckline, making a mark at the centre of each measurement. Fold along the markings.

Leaving the paper folded in half, cut along the outer pattern lines. This creates an exact mirror on both sides of the template. **(c)**

Repeat for the back pattern template.

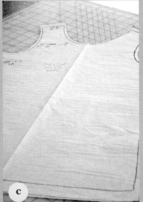

a

b

c

d

5. Modify the pattern

You can now modify the pattern. Here I will show you the modifications specific to the Little Joy Dress on page 68. Start by dividing the front dress template into 4 pieces. Draw a vertical line down the centre of the dress length – use your markings or fold line you made earlier – to divide the front into two pieces, left and right.

Next, you will divide the template again, creating 2 bodice pieces and 2 skirt pieces. Draw a horizontal line across the width of the dress front approx. 7.5–10cm (3–4in) below the armhole: 7.5cm (3in) for ages 1–2 years and 10cm (4in) for ages 3–5 years. **(d)**

Now measure from the bottom of the pattern up along the vertical centre line to the horizontal line you just drew. Make a note of this measurement to ensure that your horizontal line on the back dress template is in the exact place as the front. Repeat this process to divide the back dress template into 4 pieces.

6. Add seam allowances

The front and back templates are now divided into 4 pattern pieces each. You can now either cut out your pattern along the dividing lines and retrace it with added seam allowances, or you can add your seam allowances to the basic template as follows:

Use a different coloured pencil to distinguish your seam allowances. Measure out on both sides of your vertical centre line and the horizontal line to mark 1cm (3/8in)

seam allowances (or your preferred width) and draw a parallel line with your coloured pencil.

Now retrace each piece separately onto a fresh piece of pattern paper: the 2 bodice pieces and 2 skirt pieces including the seam allowance, so that you have 4 separate pattern pieces. Cut out the pattern pieces, transferring all notes and markings. **(e)**

Repeat for the back dress template. Add a mark to the back centre seam approx. 10cm (4in) below the neckline on each back bodice pattern piece. This shows where to begin stitching your back centre seam so the garment will fit over your child's head.

Modifying an existing pattern

A note on patterns: Many commercial pattern companies include seam allowances on their printed pattern pieces, whereas others require you to trace the patterns and add your own seam allowances. Be sure to read the pattern carefully so that you know which type you are working with.

1. Trace the pattern

Cut out the pattern in the required size and place it on top of your pattern paper. Trace the outline of the front and back pattern pieces onto your pattern paper. Alternatively, you could trace the outline of the required size onto fresh paper first, which means that you can use the pattern again in a different size. **(f)**

2. Add or adapt seam allowances

To modify a pattern that includes the seam allowance, make a note of the seam allowance used in the pattern, and add the same width seam allowance where needed to your modified pattern pieces.

This pattern included a 1.5cm (⅝in) seam allowance. For the neckline and armhole I reduced the seam allowance to my standard 6mm (¼in) to accommodate my 13mm (½in) bias tape finish.

Follow the directions from Creating a Pattern from an Existing A-line Dress or Pinafore on page 17 to apply seam allowances where needed.

This pattern requires that you cut the front dress pattern on the fold, meaning that you place the pattern on a fold (with the material doubled) creating a continuous pattern piece without a seam down the centre front. This means you need to add a seam allowance to your traced front pattern piece along the centre vertical edge, when creating block piecing.

The back dress pattern piece requires you to cut 2 of the same piece for a back centre seam, so the seam allowance is already included.

All that is left to do is to divide the pattern pieces into front and back bodice pieces, and front and back skirt pieces and add seam allowances. **(g)**

Following the same method as Creating a pattern from an existing A-line Dress or Pinafore, create your bodice and skirt pieces including seam allowances. **(h)**

When you are using your pattern pieces to mark and cut out the blocks for the pieced dress, remember to flip the front and back bodice and skirt pieces so that you have symmetrical left and right sides.

Here are a few tips that will help to give your project a professional finish. Taking a little time to finish seams or position your buttonholes and buttons correctly will pay huge dividends when you have finished the project and step back to admire your work.

Buttonholes

Consult your sewing-machine manual and test the procedure to ensure you understand the steps needed. Always do a test buttonhole on scrap fabric of the same type before starting the project.

1. Mark

To achieve the correct-size buttonhole, place the button on the fabric. Using a fabric marker, make a mark at one edge of your button and another mark on the opposite edge. **(a)**

2. Stitch

Begin stitching just above the first marking and finish the first leg of stitching just below the second marking. Continue to complete the buttonhole. **(b)**

3. Cut

Make a slit in the centre with a carefully guided seam ripper, or cut with a pair of small scissors. Avoid cutting through the end stitches. Now test the buttonhole by sliding the button through the opening. **(c)**

Clipping curves and cutting corners

When sewing rounded edges, such as necklines, clipping the curve is vital in order to achieve a smooth finish. For crisp corners, such as pockets, cut the corners.

✪ **Clip curves** After you have sewn your seam, use a pair of small scissors to make regular triangular notches in the seam allowance. Be sure not to clip through the stitching. Turn the piece right side out and press. **(d)**

✪ **Cut corners** After you have sewn your seam, cut off the point on each corner close to the stitching with sharp scissors, making sure that you do not cut through any stitches. Turn the piece right side out and push the corners out gently to achieve a neat angle. Press. **(e)**

Finishing seams

Finishing the seam allowance on a sewing project gives a professional look and will prevent woven fabrics from fraying. There are several different methods.

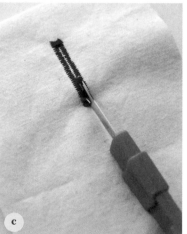

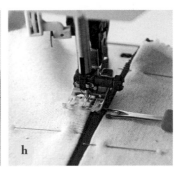

○ **Zigzag stitch method** This is quick and easy and can be achieved on any sewing machine with a zigzag stitch. After you have stitched your seam, zigzag as close to the cut edge of your seam allowance as you can, using your presser foot as a guide.

○ **Pinking shears method** This is only suitable for fabrics that do not fray easily. Use pinking shears to trim the cut edge of your seam allowance.

○ **Overlock/Serger machine method** A special overlock or serger machine is required for this finish. It works by trimming your seam allowance and finishing it at the same time with a special stitch. Some home sewing machines include a faux overlock stitch; consult your manual.

Pressing matters

Press your fabric before you cut it. Press your seams as you sew. Press carefully as you work. Press when you are finished. Pressing improves your ability to sew accurately, and creates a clean, professional look.

Zips

Zips truly are not that hard; they simply take a little practice. Here is a brief guide to sewing a simple zip without a special zip presser foot:

1. Pin carefully and then remove your pins as you sew the zip in place. **(f)**

2. Begin by opening the zip a few centimetres after you have pinned it in place. Start stitching the zip close to the folded edge of your fabric. **(g)**

3. As you approach the zip toggle, stop sewing with the needle down. Lift your presser foot and use the tip of a seam ripper to slide the zip toggle closed. Lower the presser foot and continue sewing. Repeat this process on the other side of the zip. **(h)**

Embroidery

A few basic embroidery stitches are all you need for the projects in this book.

○ **Running stitch** Bring the needle and thread to the front of the fabric. Move the needle forward along the design line to make a small straight stitch, then take the needle to the back. Bring the needle and thread to the front of the fabric a stitch length's distance from your first stitch. Make another stitch along the design line equal in length to your first stitch. Continue, keeping both the stitch length and the space between the same.

○ **Back stitch** Bring the needle and thread to the front of the fabric. Move the needle forward along the design line to make a small straight stitch. Bring the needle through to the front, a little in front of your first stitch. Stitch back to the first stitch taking your needle down at the end of your first stitch. Continue stitching along your design line.

○ **Satin stitch** Bring the needle and thread to the front at the lower edge of the design on the right. Make a straight stitch from one side to the other. Bring the needle up just above the first stitch on the right edge. Make a second straight stitch close to the first, from right to left. Continue making additional stitches close to one another so the fabric underneath is not visible. Keep stitching in this way until the shape is filled with stitches.

BOHO

For me, Boho evokes a free-spiritedness,
a sense of adventure, thoughts of travel
and summer days. Rich colours and bold
patterns play a major role in my idea of
Boho style, as do comfort and reminiscence.
I imagine strolling through colourful markets,
listening to music, dancing barefoot,
and enjoying picnics and campfires.
Here is the gypsy in me wanting to explore
and discover as much as I can, to take in
the sights, sounds and tastes of the day,
to skip and twirl and dance, and be surprised
by the world. It is from this joyful place that
the projects in this chapter were created.
Explore, be bold and find wonder!

VAGABOND BAG

The Vagabond Bag is the perfect travelling companion, whether you are shopping in the bazaars of Morocco, perusing the flea markets of Paris, carrying beach essentials in Greece, or making a trip to your local farmers' market. Its unique design allows it to fold up nice and tidy for packing, and opens up with pleated sides that add extra room for all of your treasures.

YOU WILL NEED

50 x 114cm (20 x 45in) fabric for outer bag

50 x 114cm (20 x 45in) fabric for lining

2.75m (3 yards) single-fold bias binding, 25mm (1in) wide

Thread

LEVEL

TEMPLATES

Bag opening and Bag handles (see page 139)

INSTRUCTIONS

1. Cut out the pattern pieces

Fold your main fabric in half widthways, matching the selvedge edges, right sides together.

Using the fold as the shorter top edge of the bag, cut a rectangle 40 x 50cm (15¾ x 19¾in) as shown in illustration 1. Keep your fabric folded and all raw edges aligned.

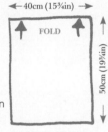

← 40cm (15¾in) →

FOLD

50cm (19¾in)

ILLUSTRATION 1

To create the handles and opening of the bag, trace one bag opening and two bag handle pattern pieces from the templates on page 139 and cut them out. Pin the templates along the top fold of the bag as shown overleaf: place the large bag opening pattern piece in the centre and pin in place (this will be the opening in the bag), then place the 2 bag handle pattern pieces at the side edges along the fold and pin in place. **(a)**

Now cut out the pattern pieces. Repeat for the lining fabric. Save the large cut-outs from the bag opening pattern piece; these will become the bag's inside pocket. **(b)**

2. Sew the inside pocket

Using the cut-out piece from your outer bag fabric, fold it with wrong sides together and pin. Stitch around all the raw edges using a 5mm (¼in) seam allowance, leaving

a 5cm (2in) opening for turning. Cut the seam allowance at the corners and clip the curves (see page 20), then turn right side out. Turn under the seam allowance at the opening and press. If you would like a sturdier pocket, use the cut-out lining piece as interfacing for your pocket. **(c)**

Now you need to pin your pocket to the right side of the lining. Centre the pocket about 10cm (4in) below the bag's large opening, then top-stitch close to the edge around the sides and bottom of the pocket, making sure to back-stitch at the beginning and end of your stitching line. **(d)**

3. Sew the bag

With right sides facing and matching the raw edges, pin the sides of your outer bag in place. Stitch along the sides of the bag, using a 1cm (⅜in) seam allowance. Repeat for the lining. Press open the seam allowances. Now turn the outer bag right sides out. Place the lining wrong side out into the outer bag, matching the seams and raw edges, and pin everything into place.

Tack the two layers together close to the raw edges along the handles and opening; this will help keep the layers from slipping around as you apply the bias binding.

Cut a length of bias binding long enough to go around the entire opening of the bag. Fold it in half along its length and

a

b

c

d

e

f

press it into a slight curve – this will help with easing it on around the curves of the handle and give a flatter finish.

Apply your bias binding along the raw edge of the bag opening, making sure that you fold the bias over the raw edges so that both the outer and lining are covered (see pages 14–15). Repeat this process for both of the handle openings. **(e)**

4. Fold the bag

Lay the bag out flat in front of you. Take the outer edge of the bag handle and fold it under until it meets the inner edge of the opening.

Now continue the fold, making a pleat down the side of the bag, adjusting as you go to keep it even, and making sure to include the lining layer in the fold. Pin in place. **(f)**

Repeat the pleating for the opposite side and press the folds in place. Tack the folds in place and along the bottom edge of the bag. To keep the folded handles from shifting you can stitch the top of the folded handle in place. **(g)**

5. Finish the bag

Now cut a length of bias binding 2.5cm (1in) longer than the width of the bottom of the bag. Again, fold the bias binding in half along its length and press. Turn under 1cm (³⁄₈in) on either end of the bias binding and press. **(h)**

Your last step is to apply the bias binding to the bottom of the bag to close the opening. Sandwich all of the layers and raw edges between the folds of the bias binding, making sure that the bias tape is folded over the raw edges encasing both the front and back of the bag (see page 14). Pin and stitch in place. **(i)**

g

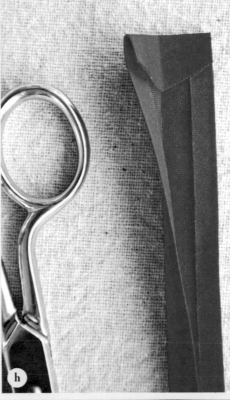

h

i

GYPSY SHIRT & JACKET

This sweet little shirt is perfect for both boys and girls from ages 3 to 10 years. It is a loose-fitting, peasant-style top that works up in light-weight woven fabrics as a free-spirited shirt, or in a heavier fabric as a jacket for cooler days. Here is the exciting part: you draft the pattern yourself! This is a great opportunity for a novice sewer to expand their skills, as well as a chance for the more experienced seamstress or tailor to add their own flair.

I have given the instructions so that you gather your measurements and cut straight into your fabric. However, the pattern could easily be made up on paper to use again and again. Once you have got the basics down, you will realize how easily the shirt makes up. Add simple pockets to the jacket version, trims and patches to the shirt version, and you will see the possibilities are endless!

YOU WILL NEED

1–1.5m x 114cm (1–1½ yards x 45in) print fabric (depending on size) – recommended fabrics for the shirt: cotton, cotton voile or linen; recommended fabrics for the jacket: corduroy, denim, furnishing-weight cotton, canvas or wool

25 x 114cm (10 x 45in) co-ordinating print fabric for plackets (see page 140)

2m (2 yards) single-fold bias tape, 1.5–2cm (⅝–¾in) wide

6 buttons

50cm (20in) elastic, 6mm (¼in) wide, for girl's sleeve cuff

Thread

Tape measure

Long ruler, such as a quilter's ruler

Fabric marker

LEVEL

NOTE

All seam allowances are 1cm (³/₈in) unless otherwise stated

INSTRUCTIONS

1. Take your child's measurements

Begin by taking a few measurements from your child (see page 16). Make a note of the following:

Shoulder width – Measure across the back at the nape of the neck from shoulder to shoulder.
Sleeve length – Ask your child to extend his or her arm straight out to the side and bend the elbow at a right angle. Measure from the shoulder over the bent elbow to the wrist.
Back neck to waist – Measure from the nape of the neck to the waist or hip; this will be the length of the shirt

so the measurement should reflect where you want the bottom of the shirt to fall on your child. If you are making up a jacket version, consider making the hem hang a little longer than you would a shirt version.

Armhole depth – Measure from the top outside edge of the shoulder down to the armpit, bring the tape measure under the armpit and back around up to the shoulder.

Once you have written down your measurements, you need to add seam allowances (SA) and fullness or hem allowances to each.

Shoulder width =	+ 2cm (¾in) SA =	+ 10cm (4in) fullness =	(A)
Back neck to waist =	+ 1cm (³/₈in) SA =	+ 2.5cm (1in) hem =	(B)
Sleeve length =	+ 1cm (³/₈in) SA =	+ 2.5cm (1in) hem =	(C)
Armhole depth =	+ 2cm (¾in) SA =	+ 15cm (6in) fullness =	(D)

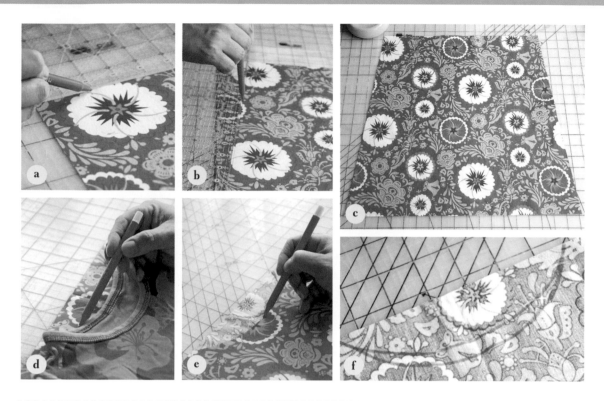

For example; the project shirt shown here is about an 8-year old girl's size. Here are the measurements I used:

Shoulder width = 35.5cm (14in)	+ 2cm (¾in) SA = 37.5cm (14¾in)	+ 10cm (4in) fullness = 47.5cm (18¾in)	(A)
Back neck to waist = 40.5cm (16in)	+ 1cm (⅜in) SA = 41.5cm (16⅜in)	+ 2.5cm (1in) hem = 44cm (17⅜in)	(B)
Sleeve length = 40.5cm (16in)	+ 1cm (⅜in) SA = 41.5cm (16⅜in)	+ 2.5cm (1in) hem = 44cm (17⅜in)	(C)
Armhole depth = 28cm (11in)	+ 2cm (¾in) SA = 30cm (11¾in)	+ 15cm (6in) fullness = 45cm (17¾in)	(D)

TIP
As your measurements of width and length may be similar, you could mark a small "W" or "L" onto the edge of the fabric pieces with a fabric marker to indicate which is which.

2. Cut your pattern pieces
Now it is time to cut your pattern pieces from the fabric. Cut two rectangles for the bodice front and back: A x B. Cut two rectangles for the sleeves: C x D. For example, using the measurements above, I cut two 47.5 x 44cm (18¾ x 17⅜in) rectangles for the bodice, and two 44 x 45cm (17⅜ x 17¾in) rectangles for the sleeves.

Lay one of your bodice pieces out in front of you; choose one long edge (the width) to be the top of the shirt – keep in mind that if your fabric has a directional pattern you will need to position the top edge accordingly. Measure and mark 5cm (2in) in from the left side, along the top edge. Repeat for the right side. **(a)**

Take your long ruler and angle it from the mark on the top edge of the left side to the bottom left corner of your fabric piece. Draw a line along the inside edge of the ruler with a fabric marker, as shown. **(b)**

Repeat for the right side. Cut along the lines you have drawn, creating a slight trapezoidal shape. **(c)**

Repeat the process above on your remaining bodice piece. Both bodice pieces should be exactly the same.

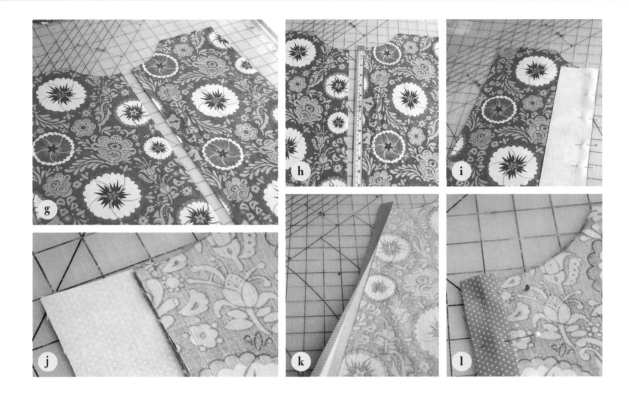

Shape the sleeves in the same manner as the bodice pieces. Lay the fabric out with the long edge (length) running vertically. Measure in 2.5cm (1in) from the left edge on the bottom (width) and make a mark along the hem edge. Repeat for the right side.

Take your long ruler and angle it from the mark on the left hem edge up to the top-left corner of the fabric and draw a line along the inside edge of the ruler with a fabric marker. Repeat for the right side. Cut along the lines you have drawn, creating a slight trapezoidal shape, narrower at the hem (cuff) end. Repeat for the remaining sleeve piece.

3. Create the bodice

Choose one of the bodice pieces to be the back of the shirt and the other to be the front. Starting with the back bodice piece, mark the centre of the top edge by folding the piece in half and pressing it. You can add a pin, or mark the fabric at this point, too.

To make the neckline, I find it works well to use one of your child's existing tops or T-shirts centred just below

the top edge of the bodice piece (mark the centre of the top and align the centre marks). Using a fabric marker, draw a line following the curve of the neckline on the top. **(d)**

Next, cut along the line you have drawn to create the back neck opening.

Place the back bodice piece on top of the front bodice piece with wrong sides facing and raw edges matching, and trace the neckline from the back bodice piece onto the front. **(e)**

Remove the back bodice piece and set aside. Draw a second, slightly deeper curved line below your first traced line onto the front bodice piece and then cut along the second line to create the front neck opening. **(f)**

Fold the front bodice piece in half, matching the raw edges, and press the length of the fold to create a centre line. Cut along the centre line to create the two front bodice panels. **(g)**

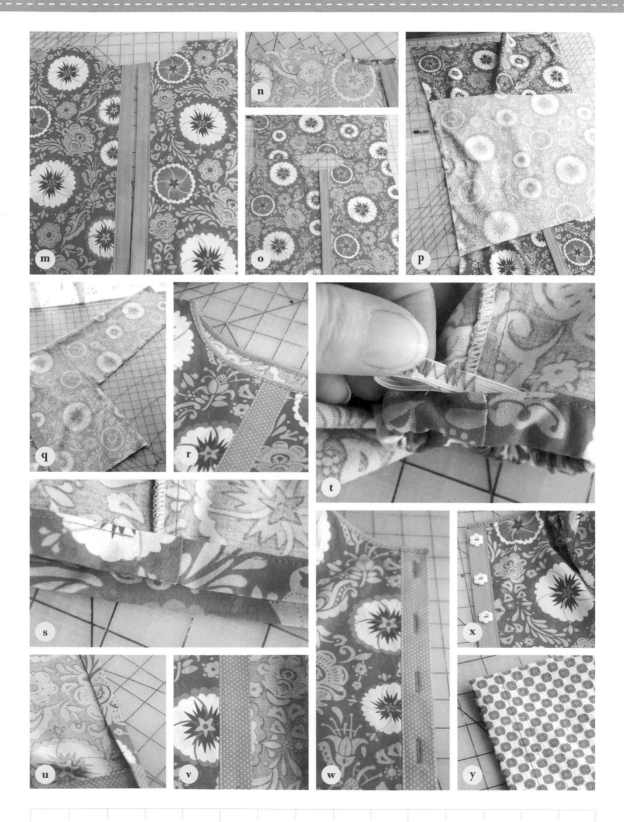

4. Add the placket strips

Measure along the cut centre line from the neckline to the bottom edge of the front bodice panel; this will be the length of your placket pieces. **(h)**

From the co-ordinating print fabric, cut two strips 7cm (2¾in) x placket length measurement. Pin one of the placket strips to the centre edge of one of the front bodice panels, right sides facing and raw edges matching. **(i)**

Next, stitch along the seam allowance, fold open the placket strip and press the seam allowance towards the placket. **(j)**

Fold over 1cm (⅜in) of the long placket raw edge and press. Fold over again by 2.5cm (1in), press and pin in place. **(k) (l)**

Stitch the placket in place close to the folded edge. Repeat the process for the remaining placket and front bodice panel. **(m)**

5. Assemble the bodice

Pin the front bodice panels to the back bodice piece at the shoulders, right sides facing and raw edges matching (overlapping the placket edges), and stitch along the seam allowances. **(n)**

Press the seam allowances open, then finish the seams in your preferred method (see page 21). Open out the front and back panels, right side up. **(o)**

6. Attach the sleeves

Find the centre of your sleeve by folding the sleeve in half with the raw edges matching and making a small mark on the centre fold on the edge opposite the narrower hem edge.

Pin one sleeve to the assembled bodice, right sides facing and matching raw edges. Align your centre mark on the shoulder seam. **(p)**

Stitch the sleeve to the bodice along the seam allowance. Repeat for the remaining sleeve and finish the seams in your preferred method.

7. Sew the seams

Fold the shirt and sleeves with right sides facing and raw edges matching. Pin the sides and the sleeve seams and stitch along the seam allowance. **(q)**

At this stage try the shirt on your child, making sure that the neckline opening is a good fit; make any adjustments needed, for example if the neckline is too tight, trim along the raw edge 1.5cm (⅝in) at a time until it fits. Bear in mind when making adjustments that the neck will be reduced by 5mm (¼in) when sewing on the bias tape.

8. Add the finishing touches

Attach bias tape or binding to the neckline (see pages 14–15), using a decorative machine stitch if you like. **(r)**

If you are making a girl's shirt, an elastic casing for the sleeve hem is a pretty finish. To create the casing, with the shirt wrong-side out, fold over 1.5cm (⅝in) of the raw edge of the sleeve and press. Fold over again by 1.5cm (⅝in), press and pin in place. Stitch close to the folded edge leaving a 4cm (1½in) opening to thread the elastic. **(s)**

Using a safety pin or bodkin attached to one end of your elastic, feed the elastic through the channel of the casing, pulling it out the other end. Adjust the elastic for fit and sew the ends of the elastic together. Stitch the opening closed. Repeat for remaining sleeve hem. **(t)**

Hem the bottom of the shirt by folding the raw edge over by 1.5cm (⅝in), pressing and folding over again by 1.5cm (⅝in). Press and pin in place. Stitch the hem close to the folded edge. **(u)**

Use a fabric marker to mark the placement of buttons and buttonholes, starting close to the neckline and then evenly spaced to approx. 2.5cm (1in) above the hemline. Stitch the buttonholes and sew on the buttons. **(v) (w) (x)**

The Gypsy Shirt is now complete!

For a boy's shirt or the jacket version, omit the elastic casing on the sleeve hem. Simply fold over 1.5cm (⅝in) of the raw edge and press. Fold over again by 1.5cm (⅝in), press and pin in place. Stitch close to the folded edge. **(y)**

As a child, there is something magical in having a special place for hiding away on a long summer's afternoon – a secret place to read, nap or daydream in a kaleidoscope of colours. Or maybe a rainy-day refuge is in order, a nook in which to foster daydreams and encourage imagination. This extraordinary patchwork tent will be the delight of the young-at-heart, no matter the age. Oh, and it's reversible, too!

YOU WILL NEED

Pattern paper or newspaper and pencil

Sticking tape

Long ruler, such as a quilter's ruler, or straight edge

3.2m x 114cm (3½ yards x 45in) bright print fabric

2.75m (3 yards) cotton twill tape

Approx. 3m (3½ yards) in total of print fabrics for patchwork in approx. 8 different patterns (about 45cm/½ yard each of 114cm/45in wide fabric pieces)

One double (full) patterned bed sheet

Thread

 LEVEL

INSTRUCTIONS

1. Make a pattern for the tent flaps

Tape together sheets of pattern paper or newspaper. With a long ruler or straight edge, draw a right-angled triangle with the following measurements: 46 x 79 x 91.5cm (18⅛ x 31 x 36in) as shown in illustration 1. Cut out the pattern piece along the drawn lines. **(a)**

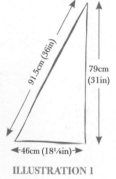

91.5cm (36in)

79cm (31in)

◄46cm (18⅛in)►

ILLUSTRATION 1

2. Cut the pattern pieces

Now cut 4 flap triangles from the print fabric. Using just over 90cm (1 yard) of fabric, fold it in half matching the selvedge edges. Pin the triangle in position and cut out 2 flaps. Reposition the triangle pattern and cut out 2 more flaps. In the photo, I have shown 2 pattern pieces to illustrate how to lay out your pattern pieces on the fabric to cut the correct 4 triangle flap pieces. **(b)**

From various print fabrics: cut twenty-four 32cm (12½in) squares for the patchwork pieces. From the cotton twill tape: cut eight 13cm (5in) lengths; four 40cm (16in) lengths. From the patterned bed sheet: cut 4 flap triangles and one 123 x 184cm (4ft x 6ft) rectangle for the reverse s   f the tent.

3. Sew the patchwork squares

Lay out the fabric squares in 6 rows of 4 and adjust the placement of the squares until you are happy with the result.

Make stacks of squares for each row in the correct order and pin together. This will help you make sure that the placement comes out as you planned when you start sewing. **(c)**

Pin together the first 2 squares of your first row, right sides together, with raw edges matching, and stitch together along one edge taking a 5mm (¼in) seam allowance. Stitch the third square to the first 2 squares and then the fourth square to complete the first row. Press all seams open. **(d)**

Continue in the same manner for the remaining 5 rows. **(e)**

Sew the rows together. Start by pinning the first and second rows together, matching seams and raw edges. Stitch the entire length of the row taking a 5mm (¼in) seam allowance and then press the seams open. Repeat to join the remaining rows.

4. Sew the outer tent

Trim 5mm (¼in) from the tip of each triangle flap piece where the long edge and hypotenuse meet. **(f)**

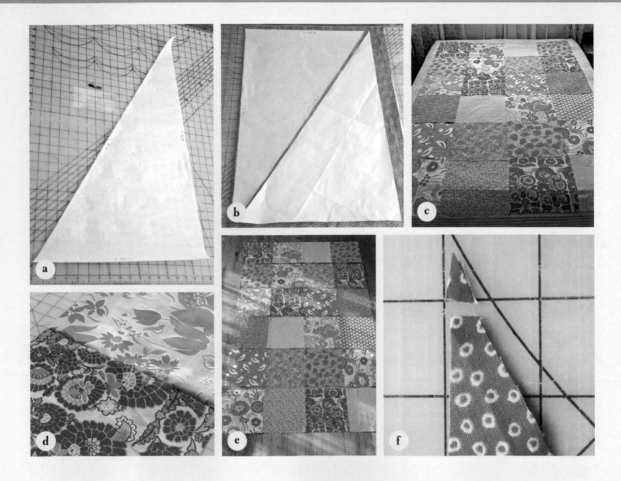

Pin the longest edge of one triangle flap piece (the hypotenuse of the right-angle triangle) to one of the long edges of your patchwork piece (across the lower 3 rows with the trimmed point at the top), right sides together, with the bottom of the triangle aligned with the corner and the tip of the triangle towards the centre of the patchwork piece, as shown. Pin in place along the outer edge. **(g)**

Repeat to position a second triangle flap piece across the upper 3 rows along the same edge, with the trimmed point opposite that of the lower flap and the top of the triangle aligned with the top corner. Pin in place along the outer edge.

Stitch along the pinned edge, taking a 1cm (³⁄₈in) seam allowance. Press the seam. Repeat this process for the 2 remaining triangle flap pieces on the opposite long edge of the patchwork piece. **(h)**

5. Sew the reverse side

Sew the reverse side triangle flap pieces to the reverse side of the large rectangle along the long edges, as described above.

Fold the short lengths of twill tape in half to create a loop. Following illustration 2, pin 3 loops along one short edge of the rectangle: one in the centre and one on each triangle flap seam. Tack in place.

Repeat with 3 more loops along the other short edge. Pin the remaining loops centred between the triangle flap pieces on both long sides of the rectangle and tack in place. **(i)**

Take the 4 long lengths of twill tape and tack one end to the centre of the long raw edge of each 4 triangle flap pieces. These will be the tent flap ties. **(j)**

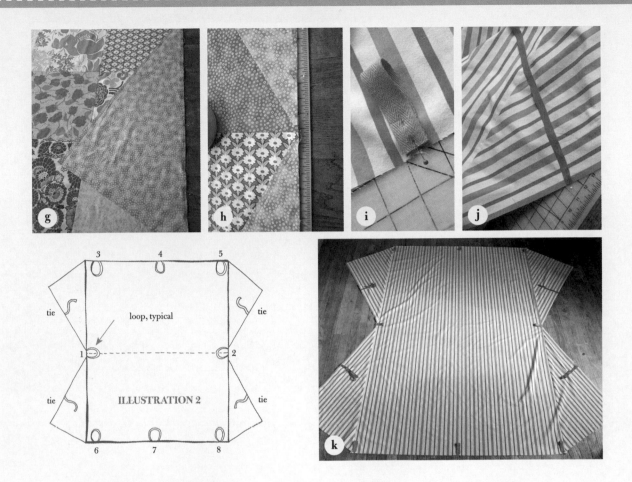

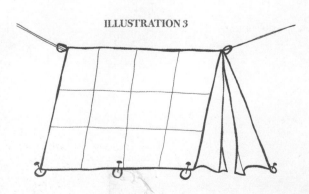

ILLUSTRATION 2

loop, typical

tie

tie

tie

tie

ILLUSTRATION 3

6. Sew the tent

Lay out the reverse side of the tent (the bedsheet) with the right side facing up and place the patchwork side of the tent on top so that the right sides are together. Match all the raw edges and pin around the entire tent. **(k)**

Machine stitch all edges using a 1cm (³⁄₈in) seam allowance, leaving an opening of about 15cm (6in) for turning. Turn the tent right side out, turn under the seam allowance at the opening, and press the entire tent. Top stitch around all the edges; this will close the opening.

7. Set up the tent

To set up your beautiful tent: thread rope or sturdy string through both of the centre loops and tie it to trees or poles. Secure the bottom-side loops with tent spikes or weights, as shown in illustration 3. Now pull in a blanket, a cosy cushion and a few of your favourite books!

BOHO BATH MAT

In making for my home, I find the most oft-neglected room of the Little Green Cottage to be the bathroom. To remedy this I created this happy project – a bit of bright and cheerful to make you smile. Imagine stepping out of the bath or shower with your squeaky clean toes landing upon a soft, cosy and very happy Boho Bath Mat. How nice!

I have chosen bright colours with a bit of a punch; you may choose to use fabrics that co-ordinate with your own colour scheme. I have also found this happy mat works very well in the kitchen, too.

YOU WILL NEED

25 x 114cm (10 x 45in) each of 4 different cotton print fabrics

1 towelling bath towel

Thread

LEVEL

NOTE

All seam allowances are 1cm (³⁄₈in) unless otherwise stated.

INSTRUCTIONS

1. Prepare the fabrics

From the 4 different fabrics, cut a total of nine 10 x 14cm (4 x 5½in) rectangles (A) and eighteen 10 x 22cm (4 x 8¾in) rectangles (B). From the bath towel, cut a 76 x 55cm (30 x 21¾in) rectangle.

2. Arrange the pieces

Lay out the print fabric rectangles to find the most pleasing combination. The pattern is similar to a brickwork layout: begin with a 10 x 14cm (4 x 5½in) rectangle (A) for the first row followed by 2 of the longer 10 x 22cm (4 x 8¾in) rectangles (B), working vertically (ABB). For the second row, begin with 2 longer rectangles, followed by a smaller rectangle (BBA). Alternate between the 2 row arrangements for the remaining 7 rows, as shown in illustration 1.

3. Sew the rows

Once you have your final layout ready, begin sewing the vertical rows. Starting with the first row, place the 10 x 14cm (4 x 5½in) rectangle (A) right sides together with the following 10 x 22cm (4 x 8¾in) rectangle (B), raw edges matching. Pin the short edge in place and stitch along the seam allowance.

Attach the remaining B rectangle from the first row to the rectangles you have just sewn by placing it right side

row 1	row 2	row 3	row 4	row 5	row 6	row 7	row 8	row 9
a	b	a	b	a	b	a	b	a
b	b	b	b	b	b	b	b	b
b	a	b	a	b	a	b	a	b

ILLUSTRATION 1

together with the previous B rectangle, matching raw edges. Pin along the short edge and stitch along the seam allowance. Press the seams open. This is your completed first row. **(a)**

Sew the second row in the same manner, starting with the first two B rectangles and finishing with the remaining A rectangle. Repeat this process for the remaining rows, following the alternate sequence.

Place the first two rows together, right sides facing and raw edges matching. Pin along the long edge. Stitch together along the seam allowance and press the seams open. **(b)**

Repeat this process for the remaining rows to complete the bath mat top.

4. Attach the backing

Lay the pieced bath mat top right side up on your work surface. Place the towelling rectangle piece on top of the patchwork piece with right sides facing and matching raw edges. Trim the raw edges of both the towel and pieced top even with each other, if necessary. Smooth both pieces free of any wrinkles and pin in place around all edges.

Stitch around all of the edges, leaving a 15cm (6in) opening for turning. Turn the bath mat right side out. Fold under the seam allowances at the opening and press the entire mat neatly.

Top-stitch close to the edge around all sides of the mat; this will give a nice finished look, and will also close up the opening.

SKIPPING SKIRT

While watching my daughter play in the garden, I was struck by the sheer joy and enthusiasm with which she threw herself into every action. The simple pleasures of childhood are abundant; long summer evenings staying up late, running through sprinklers, bedtime stories, jumping, twirling and skipping with abandon. The Skipping Skirt celebrates that feeling with the perfect amount of twirl for spinning and lots of swing for skipping.

TIP

Look through your scrap pile for unique pieces that you love and use them all together for a mix 'n' match freestyle approach. This skirt works up beautifully in vintage linens, or in heavier fabrics, such as wool flannel or corduroy for colder climes.

YOU WILL NEED

Girl's skirt sizes: 5/6 years, 7/8 years & 9/10 years

Pattern paper or newspaper and pencil

Long ruler (a quilter's ruler is perfect)

Approx. 90cm (1 yard) in total of mixed fabrics such as cotton, voile, shirting, corduroy, denim (about 25cm/ ¼ yard each of 114cm/45in wide fabric pieces)

Elastic, 19mm (¾in) wide

Thread

Bias binding (optional)

LEVEL

INSTRUCTIONS

1. Draw the pattern

The main pattern piece required for the skirt is a tall trapezoid. The skirt length is the only measurement that differs between sizes (the waist is adjusted to fit with elastic). This example shows the girl's size 7/8: see below for measurements for all sizes.

Place your paper on a flat surface. Near the bottom edge of your paper take your ruler and draw a horizontal line 15cm (6in) in length. From the centre of your horizontal line, draw a vertical line up at a length of:

- ✪ Size 5/6: 33cm (13in)
- ✪ Size 7/8: 38cm (15in)
- ✪ Size 9/10: 43cm (17in)

Next, centred at the top of your vertical line, draw a horizontal line 7.5cm (3in) long. Now that you have all of your measurements and your first 3 lines drawn, take your long ruler and place it at the ends of your top and bottom horizontal lines; draw angled lines connecting them. **(a)** Cut out the pattern from the paper – you now have your completed pattern piece.

2. Cut the pieces

Pin your prepared pattern piece to your chosen fabrics and cut out fourteen pieces. In this example, I used 5 different fabrics. **(b)**

For the waistband, cut one strip of fabric measuring 7.5 x 96.5cm (3 x 38in). You may also piece the waistband, if you like. **(c)**

3. Sew the skirt

You may want to take a moment to play with your fabric pieces, laying them out to find a pleasing arrangement. Once you have a plan, take your first 2 skirt pieces and place them right sides together, matching raw edges, and pin along one side. **(d)**

Sew the pieces together along the pinned side using a 1cm (⅜in) seam allowance, making sure to back stitch at the beginning and end of your stitching line. Pick up your next piece and place it right side facing the second piece of your stitched section, with raw edges matching. Pin along the seam allowance and stitch in the same manner as the first seam.

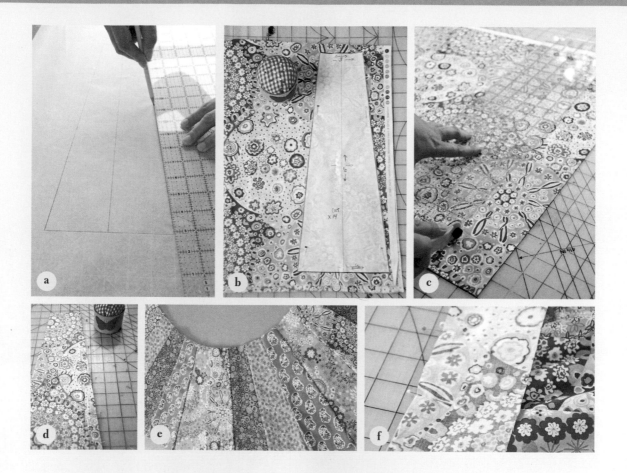

Continue stitching in the same way with the remaining pieces. Do not close the final seam. Finish your seam allowances in your preferred method (see page 21) and press all of your seam allowances to one side. **(e)**

4. Attach the waistband

Now that you have your skirt pieces all sewn, the next step is to attach the waistband. Begin by pinning one end of the waistband to one end of the top of your skirt, right sides together with raw edges matching. As you pin, you will want to slightly ease the top of the skirt into a straighter edge (as the skirt has a natural curve); this will make the waistband fit the top of the skirt better. Pin the waistband along the entire top of the skirt. **(f)**

It is likely that you will have some extra length of waistband extending past the top of the skirt. I have included this purposefully to allow for the variable give of different

fabrics. Simply trim the excess from the waistband to match the raw edge of the top of the skirt. **(g)**

Stitch the waistband to the skirt using a 1cm (3/8in) seam allowance. Press the seam allowance towards the waistband.

Sew your final skirt seam by folding the skirt in half with right sides together and raw edges matching. Pin along the seam allowance and stitch 1cm (3/8in) from the top of the waistband to the bottom of your skirt.

Finish the seam allowance in your preferred method (see page 21) and press.

5. Finish the waistband

Begin by folding over 1cm (3/8in), wrong sides together, along the top edge of your waistband and pressing

into place. Fold over again by 3cm (1 1/8 in) and press into place again. Pin the waistband to the skirt along the folded edge. **(h)**

Stitch your waistband to the skirt 3mm (1/8 in) from the folded edge, making sure to leave a 5cm (2in) opening for inserting elastic. Alternatively, once you have pinned your waistband down, you could turn the skirt to the right side and "stitch in the ditch" of the waistband seam (see Glossary, page 140).

To determine the length of elastic you need for your skirt, call out to your child to "just come here for a quick second!" and hope that they will stand still for a half a minute. Wrap the elastic around their natural waist so that it is snug while comfortable, and then add about 2.5cm (1in) to that length. Now insert the elastic into the waistband casing using a bodkin or safety pin: attach one end of elastic to

the bodkin and push it into the casing. Keep feeding it through the channel until it reappears at the other end. Pull the elastic through and remove the bodkin.

Overlap the ends of your elastic by about 1cm (3/8 in) and stitch together. Now you can stitch the opening in the waistband casing closed. **(i)**

6. Finish the hem

To finish your skirt, you can create a narrow hem by folding over 5mm (1/4 in) twice, pressing into place, pinning and stitching close to the folded edge. You could also finish the hem with some bias-binding tape, or even a sweet ruffle. **(j)**

Now you are finished! Hold up your masterpiece and admire for a moment before the little girl of the house runs off with it for skipping and twirling practice!

3

NATURAL

I find so much inspiration in the natural
world: the variations in texture, pattern
and colour. The play of light and shadow
upon the everyday landscape fascinates me.
I often find that if I am stuck for ideas or
blocked in my creativity, a walk under tall
trees, or along the edge of the ocean, or a
stroll through the garden – anywhere I can be
out in the natural elements – can change my
perspective and spur me on to create in ways
unexpected. A moment outside can revitalize
my thought process. Take or make a bag to
collect any treasures that inspire you on your
walks – shells, stones, feathers and leaves –
and bring the outside in.

53 54 55 56 57 58 59 60

When I was young, my family and I lived along a winding river, our house tucked up on a hillside in the woods. I remember that all of my free time was spent wandering those woods. I knew every trail, every secret spot, and every place that the wild flowers grew. I would come home from my adventures with my arms full and decorate our house with flowers in every nook and cranny. I love these Pockets Full of Posies made from linen and bits of vintage finery – perfect for wild flowers. They also make wonderful storage for pens, pencils or paintbrushes in a workspace.

YOU WILL NEED

Linen scraps for the outer shell, approx. 25 x 36cm (10 x 14in)

Cotton scraps for the lining, approx. 25 x 36cm (10 x 14in)

Light- or medium-weight fusible interfacing

Embellishments, such as vintage linen napkins, doilies and ribbon

Thread

Buttons (one per pocket)

Jam jar, glass bottle or other waterproof vessel

Curtain or towel rod, for hanging

 LEVEL

INSTRUCTIONS

1. Prepare the pattern pieces

Cut one 25 x 18cm (10 x 7in) rectangle each from the linen, cotton and interfacing. These will become the vase. Cut one 8 x 18cm (3 x 7in) rectangle each from the linen, cotton and interfacing. These will become the handle. In this example, I cut a corner triangle from a vintage linen napkin for embellishment. You could use a sweet vintage hankie, a bit of doily, embroidery, ribbon and buttons… anything that strikes your fancy, really.

Following the manufacturer's instructions, fuse the corresponding interfacing to the wrong side of each of your lining pieces, then set aside.

2. Embellish the piece

Take your large linen rectangle and your embellishments; choose one long edge to be the top of your fabric vase and sew the embellishments to your linen piece. Set aside. **(a)**

3. Sew the handle

Place the smaller linen and lining pieces right sides together, matching raw edges. Pin in place. Stitch around three sides with a 1cm (³/8 in) seam allowance, leaving one narrow end of the rectangle open. Trim the seam allowance and clip the corners. Turn the handle right side out and press. Top-stitch 5mm (¼in) around the 3 sewn edges.

Create a buttonhole centred on the sewn end of the handle, the appropriate size for your button (see page 20). **(b)**

4. Sew the outer vase

To create the vase, take your embellished linen rectangle and fold it in half, short sides matching and right sides together. Pin. Stitch along the raw edges taking a 1cm (³/8in) seam allowance. Press the seam open and fold the vase in order to centre the seam. This seam will be the back of your vase.

Stitch along the bottom edge of your piece using a 1cm (³/8in) seam allowance. Clip the corners and press the seam open. **(c)**

This next stage is a little like origami and can seem a bit tricky if you have never done boxed corners before; just take a deep breath and let it come naturally. Working with the bottom seam of the vase, pinch/pull the corners into triangles, making sure they are even and centred, then press the triangles so they are nice and crisp. You want to fold the bottom of your vase into a kind of square, making sure everything is centred properly, as shown. **(d)**

Using a pencil or fabric marker, make a mark 2.5cm (1in) in from the corners on the bottom seam on both ends.

Using a straight edge or quilter's ruler, draw a line through your markings. **(e)**

Secure your triangles with pins and stitch along the lines you have drawn. Trim off the excess of the triangle near the stitch line and press.

TIP
Use a rolled up hand towel inside tight spaces to help with pressing.

5. Sew the lining
Take your large interfaced lining rectangle and fold it in half, with short sides matching and right sides together. Pin. Stitch along the raw edges with a 1cm (⅜in) seam allowance, making sure to leave a 5cm (2in) opening in the seam for turning.

Continue sewing the lining piece, following step 4 instructions for the outer vase. Turn right side out.

6. Finish the vase
With the outer vase the wrong side out, centre the handle inside on the back seam, matching the raw edges. Pin and tack in place. **(f)**

Tuck the lining, with the right side out, into the outer vase, aligning the back seams and matching the raw edges. Pin the lining in place. Stitch 1cm (⅜in) around the raw edges. **(g)**

Turn the vase the right side out through the lining opening. Stitch the opening closed using your preferred method. Tuck the lining down into the outer vase and press it neatly. **(h)**

Measure and mark approx. 9cm (3½in) down from the top of the vase on the back seam. **(i)** Stitch your button in place on the mark. **(j)**

Place a jam jar, glass bottle, or other waterproof vessel inside the fabric shell and you have your finished fabric wall vase! Using a curtain or towel rod attached to the wall, hang your vase by the handle and button up. Use 2 or 3 in a row for a dramatic effect. All that is left to do is to fill your vase with some lovely flowers and enjoy!

7. Variation
If you would like to make a posy vase to hang on a hook instead of a curtain rod, bypass making the handle and replace it with a length of ribbon folded into a loop. Attach it in the same way you would the handle (see step 6). **(k)** …and Ta Da!

When I see a beautiful sunset or an awe-inspiring view I often wish I were a painter so that I could capture the scene and the feeling. Why not paint with fabric? Yes, you can sew art!

Simple sewn canvases can make a big statement. You can hang your one-of-a-kind art pieces in pride of place on the walls of your home. The following examples were inspired by the natural world; however, the applications and ideas are limitless. Experiment with different shapes, colours and textures to create more original pieces, or try a no-sew option by using a stencil and fabric paint. This is such a great project for playing with colour and texture, so let your imagination be your guide.

YOU WILL NEED

Small, colourfast fabric scraps (I used some silk dupion) in different colours or shades, depending on your design

Water-soluble stabilizer fabric, such as Aquafilm Solvy

Background fabric, such as linen (enough to fit your canvas board plus extra to wrap around the edges, I used a sand-coloured linen)

A bowl and water

Ready-made artist canvas (I used 30.5cm/12in square)

Heavy-duty staple gun and staples, or upholstery tacks

Embroidery thread, buttons or other embellishment

Thread – use a few different colours or shades to create lots of interest

LEVEL

INSTRUCTIONS

1. Prepare your fabric pieces
Cut the fabric scraps into small squares and rectangles – they don't have to be exactly the same size or regular shapes, the more organic the better! **(a)**

Cut a piece of the water-soluble stabilizer fabric slightly larger than the size of your desired design.

Cut a square or rectangle from your background fabric large enough to wrap around the edges of your canvas. My canvas was 30.5cm (12in) square, so I cut my fabric into a 40cm (16in) square.

Play around with your scraps until you have an idea of how you want them to look. Think about colour placement, if you want clean lines or uneven edges, and the overall composition. Once you have this in mind, start sewing!

2. Sew the design
Place one square or rectangle of fabric on the top edge of the stabilizer. Stitch on the fabric, keeping the needle in the fabric once you have finished. Place your next scrap below the first and stitch in place. Continue in this manner until you have one complete row of stitched scraps. **(b)**

Begin a second row, continuing in the same way as with the first. Overlap some of the scraps; place some horizontally, some vertically; whatever makes you happy. Repeat the process for a third row and continue until you have completed your piece. **(c)**

TIP
You can make up your design and pin your scraps to the stabilizer fabric before stitching, just be sure to remove the pins as you go to avoid catching your needle or presser foot on them.

3. Completing the design
Take the pieced design and run lines of stitching both vertically and horizontally across all the pieces, making a loose grid. This is a great time to use different colours of thread. You want to do quite a few runs in both directions so that your piece stays cohesive and will not twist. **(d)**

Fill a bowl with water and place the stitched stabilizer fabric in it to soak for a couple of minutes. This will dissolve most of the stabilizer. Rinse the piece under running water and pat dry any excess water with a towel. Lay the piece flat to dry thoroughly. **(e)**

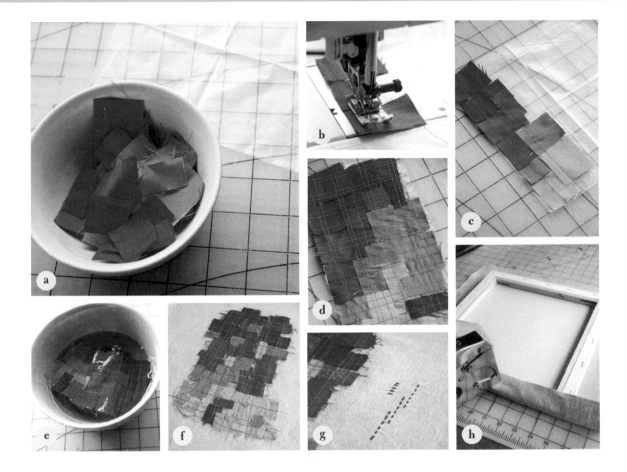

Once your piece is dry, you can press it with an iron. I liked the wrinkled look of mine, so I only pressed it minimally.

4. Sew on to the background fabric

Place your design piece wrong side down on the right side of the background fabric. Pin in place. Using rows of vertical and horizontal stitches, sew the design piece to the background. **(f)**

You can leave it as is, or add some other elements to the piece. Some simple embroidery, like a running stitch, is striking; or add buttons or other embellishment. **(g)**

5. Attach to the canvas

Place your sewn piece face down on a flat sturdy surface, and place the ready-made canvas face down, centred on top of the sewn piece. Starting with one edge of the sewn fabric piece, wrap the excess fabric around to the back of the canvas and staple (or use upholstery tacks) to the frame of the canvas along one side. Start in the centre and work out to one edge, then from the centre out in the opposite direction. **(h)**

Working from the opposite side of the stapled edge, pull the fabric taut and staple it to the frame. Check the front of your piece occasionally to make sure you are not pulling too tightly, causing the fabric to stretch out of shape. Repeat for the two remaining edges. Fold over the fabric corners and staple to the back of the frame.

You now have a gorgeous, original work of art to hang in your home!

A-gathering we will go! This roomy over-the-shoulder bag is perfect for a day's adventure. Whether you are an amateur naturalist gathering botanicals and making field notes on a trek through the forest, an urban explorer hunting for the perfect thrifty treasure, or perhaps a parent carrying all of the essentials, this Gathering Bag holds everything you need while at the same time being rather stylish.

YOU WILL NEED

50 x 114cm (20 x 45in) plain cotton fabric for the main body

25 x 114cm (10 x 45in) contrasting plain cotton fabric for the side pieces

50 x 114cm (20 x 45in) print cotton fabric for the lining

50 x 114cm (20 x 45in) contrasting print cotton for the flap, pocket and strap

Medium-weight fusible interfacing

CD or saucer for template

Fabric marker

One large button (optional)

Thread

LEVEL

NOTE

All seam allowances are 1cm (³⁄₈in) unless otherwise stated

INSTRUCTIONS

1. Prepare the fabrics

From the plain fabric: cut two 33 x 37cm (13 x 14½in) rectangles for the main body and two 7 x 51cm (2¾ x 20in) strips for the side from contrasting plain fabric, if you wish.

From the lining fabric: cut two 33 x 37cm (13 x 14½in) rectangles for the main body; two 7 x 51cm (2¾ x 20in) strips for the side; one 27 x 33cm (10½ x 13in) rectangle for the pocket; one 20 x 33cm (8 x 13in) rectangle for the flap; two 7 x 58.5cm (2¾ x 23in) strips for the strap.

From the contrasting print fabric: cut one 27 x 33cm (10½ x 13in) rectangle for the pocket; one 20 x 33cm (8 x 13in) rectangle for the flap; two 7 x 58.5cm (2¾ x 23in) strips for the strap.

From the interfacing: cut two 33 x 37cm (13 x 14½in) rectangles for the main body; two 7 x 51cm (2¾ x 20in)

strips for the sides; one 27 x 33cm (10½ x 13in) rectangle for pocket; one 20 x 33cm (8 x 13in) rectangle for the flap; two 7 x 58.5cm (2¾ x 23in) strips for the strap.

Begin by fusing the interfacing to the corresponding lining pieces, following the manufacturer's instructions.

Gather the exterior rectangles for the main body, pocket and flap pieces, as well as the lining rectangles for the main body, pocket and flap pieces. Round the bottom 2 corners of each rectangle along one 33cm (13in) edge (if you are using a directional print fabric check carefully which is the "bottom" edge), using a CD or a small saucer as a template. Align the CD, or saucer, at the corner, then use a fabric marker to trace around the curve. **(a)**

Cut along the curved line and repeat for the opposite bottom corner. Round the bottom corners of the remaining pieces in the same manner. **(b)**

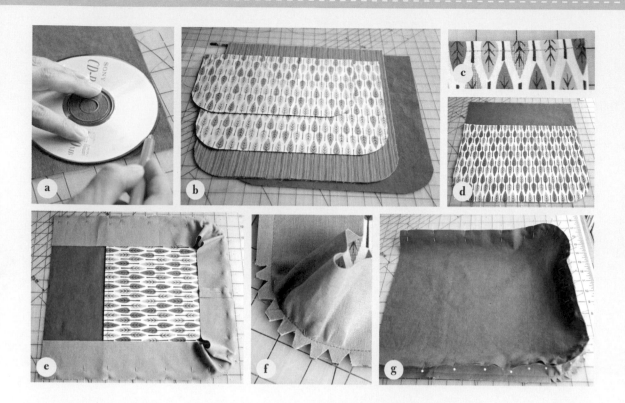

2. Attach the pocket

Place the exterior contrasting print 27 x 33cm (10½ x 13in) rectangle pocket piece together with the corresponding lining pocket piece, right sides facing and raw edges matching. Pin and stitch along the top seam allowance. Turn the pieces right side out with wrong sides facing, raw edges matching, and press. Finish by top-stitching along the top edge. **(c)**

Pin the finished pocket to one of the exterior main bag pieces, with the wrong side of the pocket facing the right side of the exterior piece, matching the rounded raw edges. Pin then tack in place. **(d)**

3. Assemble the main body

Place the two 7 x 51cm (2¾ x 20in) main body strips together, right sides facing and raw edges matching. Pin the strips along one of the short edges and stitch along the seam allowance. Press the seam allowance open.

Carefully pin the side strip to the exterior bag and pocket piece, right sides facing and raw edges matching. **(e)**

Stitch along the pinned edge. As you reach the rounded corners stitch slowly, using your fingers to manipulate any excess fabric and move any wrinkles, puckers or gathers out of the line of stitching. Clip notches along the seam allowance at the curves as shown, making sure not to cut through any stitches. **(f)**

Pin the remaining exterior bag piece to the raw edge of the side strip. Stitch and clip the curves as before. Turn the bag body right side out and press neatly. **(g)**

Turn the bag wrong side out again and set aside.

4. Sew the lining

Sew the bag lining in the same manner as the exterior, making sure to leave a 10–13cm (4–5in) opening for turning along one bottom seam. **(h)**

5. Sew the flap and straps

Pin together the contrasting print 20 x 33cm (8 x 13in) flap piece with the corresponding lining flap piece, right sides facing and raw edges matching. Stitch around

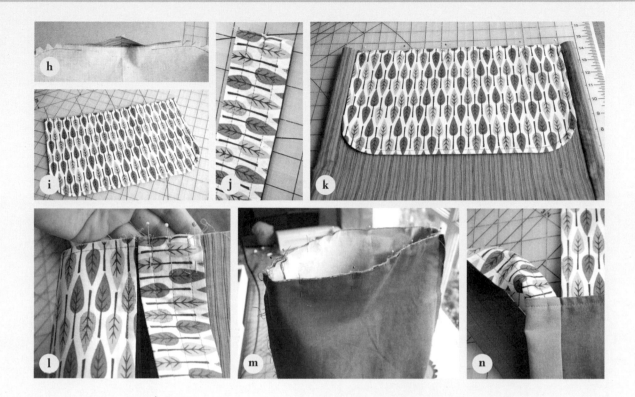

the sides and curved bottom edges, leaving the top unstitched. Turn the flap right side out, press, and top-stitch around the sewn edges. **(i)**

For the strap, pin together the two contrasting print 7 x 58.5cm (2¾ x 23in) strips along one short edge, right sides facing, raw edges matching, stitch along the pinned edge and press the seam open. Repeat to join the strips for the strap lining. Pin the strap exterior to the strap lining, right sides facing and raw edges matching. Stitch along the 2 long edges leaving the short ends open. Turn the strap right side out and press. To finish the strap, sew 3 lines of top stitching along the length of the strap. **(j)**

6. Assemble the bag
Turn the bag lining right side out. Pin the bag flap to one side of the bag lining, with the wrong side of the flap facing the right side of the lining, raw edges matching. Tack in place. **(k)**

Pin the bag strap ends to the sides of the bag lining with the wrong side of the strap facing the right side of the lining, raw edges matching, and tack in place. **(l)**

Slide the bag lining inside the bag exterior (which is wrong side out). As you do this, make sure that the lining side with the flap attached faces the exterior side with the pocket, and that the flap and straps are safely tucked inside. Pin the exterior and lining together along the top edge, matching seams and raw edges. **(m)**

Stitch around the entire pinned top edge of the bag. Reach through the opening in the lining to pull the bag right side out. Turn under the seam allowance at the opening and stitch the opening closed either by hand using a slip stitch (see page 140), or by machine using a straight stitch close to the folded edges of the seam allowance. Tuck the lining into the bag exterior and press the entire bag neatly. Top-stitch along the top edge of the bag, making sure not to catch the flap or straps in your stitching. **(n)**

To add a finishing touch you could sew a big button to the flap – this is optional as it has no function, it just looks kind of groovy.

Now, go a-gathering with your handsome Gathering Bag!

In the great forest among the tall trees, if you are very quiet and very still, you might be lucky enough to catch a glimpse of the King of the Forest, the Wild Stag. Should you move or make a sound, in a flash he will bound away, heading deep into the wilderness.

This cushion cover brings the woods inside with fabrics in greens and neutrals. Combining crisp prints with a bit of lace and ribbon adds texture and interest. It features an eye-catching, majestic leaping stag silhouette that you can easily create using a stencil and fabric paint.

YOU WILL NEED

Approx. 1m (1 yard) in total of different fabrics: 45cm (½ yard) main print fabric; 25cm (10in) contrasting print fabric (A); 25cm (10in) light-coloured plain fabric; approx. 15 x 23cm (6 x 9in) scrap of contrasting print fabric (B)

Freezer paper

Craft knife or small scissors

Fabric paint

Foam brush

23cm (9in) lace, approx. 5cm (2in) wide

46cm (½ yard) ribbon, approx. 5mm (¼in) wide

2 buttons

Thread

40cm (16in) cushion pad

LEVEL

TEMPLATES

Leaping stag (see page 136)

NOTE

All seam allowances are 1.3cm (½in) unless otherwise stated

INSTRUCTIONS

1. Prepare your materials

For the front of the cushion: cut one 21.5 x 34.5cm (8½ x 13½in) light-coloured rectangle; one 25.5 x 44.5cm (10 x 17½in) main print rectangle; one 14 x 21.5cm (5½ x 8½in) contrasting print rectangle (B); one 21.5cm (8½in) length of lace; one 44.5cm (17½in) length of ribbon.

For the back of the cushion: cut two 33 x 44.5cm (13 x 17½in) rectangles, one in main fabric, one in contrasting print (A).

2. Paint the stencil

Transfer the Leaping stag template on page 136 to freezer paper and carefully cut out with small scissors. **(a)**

Place the stag stencil on the light-coloured rectangle and paint the stencil following the instructions on page 13. **(b)**

Remove the template and let the paint dry and set according to the manufacturer's instructions.

3. Sew the front cover

Place the small contrasting print rectangle along the bottom edge of the stencilled piece, right sides together and raw edges matching. **(c)** Pin. Stitch together and press the seam.

Pin the length of lace on the print fabric, right side up, matching one edge along the seam. **(d)**

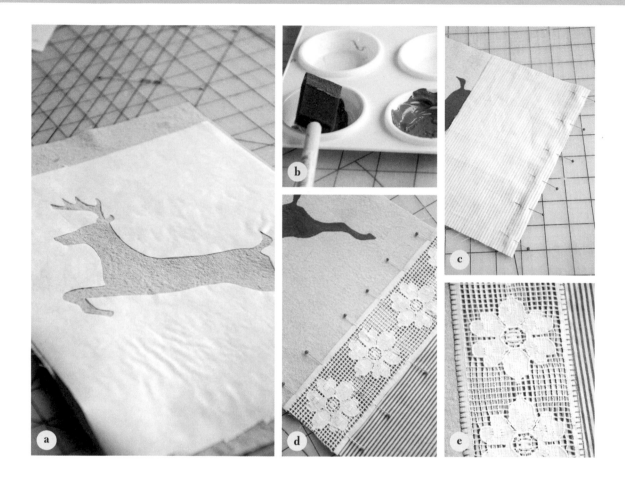

Stitch in place along both edges. Try to use a slightly decorative stitch, if your sewing machine has the option. I've used a blanket stitch (see Glossary, page 140) in contrasting thread. **(e)**

Place the stencilled panel on top of the large print rectangle, right sides facing and matching raw edges. Pin along the seam allowance as shown, stitch and press the seam. **(f) (g)**

Position the length of ribbon along your freshly pressed seam on the front and pin it in place. Stitch the entire length of ribbon. I used a wide zigzag stitch for the narrow ribbon. **(h)**

Add a couple of woodsy buttons in natural colours to decorate your cushion (see page 11). Now the front of your cushion is complete! **(i)**

4. Sew the back cover

Fold over 2.5cm (1in) along the long edge of one rectangle, fold it over by another 2.5cm (1in) to create a double hem. Pin in place and stitch close to the folded edge. Repeat for the remaining rectangle.

Lay the front cushion piece right side up on your work surface. Place one of the back panels on top, aligned with one side edge, right sides facing and raw edges matching. Pin. Place the second back panel on top along the opposite side edge and pin. **(j) (k)**

Stitch around all of the raw edges, turn right side out through the back opening and press. Now dress your cushion pad in the majesty that is the King of the Forest!

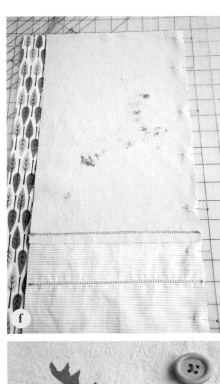

f

g

h

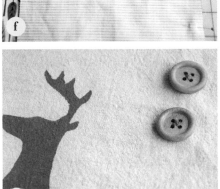

i

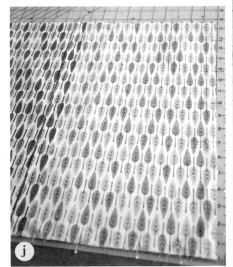

j

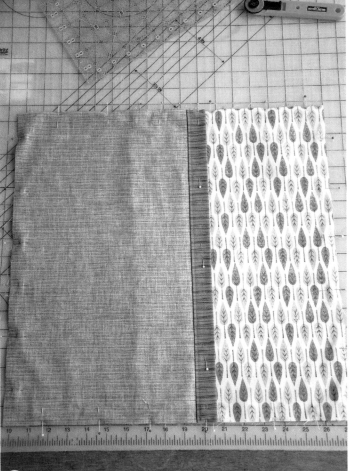

k

This woodsy throw blanket is just the thing to keep you cosy on a chilly day. Done up in muted earth tones and shades of green, with hand-printed woodland critters, it seems almost enchanted.

I have used some lovely cotton/linen blend fabric for the front of the throw, and a wool blanket I found in a second-hand shop for the backing. It would make up well using quilting-weight cottons for the front, and any wool, corduroy or even fleece for the backing.

In this example, I have printed 12 squares with woodland creatures and left 13 squares plain. Feel free to use any combination you like!

YOU WILL NEED

50 x 114cm (20 x 45in) each of fabric in the following colours: forest green; olive green; chocolate brown; natural; cream

Wool blanket or approx. 1.8m (2 yards) fabric, 152cm (60in) wide

Freezer paper

Fabric paint

Foam paintbrush

Thread

LEVEL

TEMPLATES

Fox, Hare, Buck, Bear, Crow, Doe, Owl, Wolf, Eagle, Squirrel, Stag head, and Fir trees (see pages 132–5)

NOTE

Finished size approx. 150 x 150cm (59 x 59in)

INSTRUCTIONS

1. Prepare the stencils and fabric

Prepare all freezer-paper stencils using the templates on pages 132–5, following the techniques on page 13.

Cut five 27cm (10.5in) squares from each of the fabrics, giving a total of 25 squares. Lay out the squares in 5 rows of 5. Move them around until you are happy with the balance and layout. **(a)**

Next, decide how you would like to place the printed squares and where you would like the different animals to go. Once this is done, stack the first row of squares 1–5 and pin together. Repeat for the following rows and place them in order.

TIP

I find it helpful to sketch a quick 5 x 5 grid, with notes of colour order and animal placement in each square. That

way, if I have to leave the project for a couple of days, I don't have to rely on my memory alone and can use this as a handy guide when I return to it.

2. Paint the stencils

Prepare your squares to be printed with the freezer-paper stencils, and paint all of the animals following the techniques on page 13. **(b)**

Once your stencilled squares have dried and you have set the fabric paint according to the manufacturer's instructions, it is time to assemble the throw top.

3. Assemble the rows

Begin by placing the first 2 squares from Row 1 together, right sides facing and edges matching. Pin. Double check that you have the pinned edge where you want the seam to go; do this by opening up your squares

after you have pinned them to see that the printed square is right side up, and in the correct order.

Stitch the squares together using a 5mm (¼in) seam allowance. Place the third square from Row 1 together with the second square you have just sewn, right sides together and edges matching. Pin in place and stitch. **(c)**

Continue in the same manner for the remainder of the squares for Row 1. Press all seam allowances open. Repeat this process for the 4 remaining rows. **(d)**

4. Assemble the top

Once all of the rows are complete, begin sewing the rows together. Start with Rows 1 and 2, placing them together with right sides facing and edges matching, again making sure of the correct placement. Pin. Stitch the rows together using a 5mm (¼in) seam allowance. Press the seams open. **(e)**

Continue in the same manner for all of the remaining rows until all 5 rows are stitched together. Press the entire throw top smooth.

5. Sew the back

Lay the wool blanket or fabric out with right side facing up; make sure the blanket is as smooth and flat as possible.

Next, lay the completed throw on top of the wool blanket, right side facing down, so that the blanket and the top of the throw have right sides together. The blanket should be bigger than the quilt top and extend beyond it on all sides. Smooth both layers so that there are no bumps or wrinkles and both lie flat.

Secure both layers together with a pin in the centre of each square; this will keep them from shifting while you work. Carefully cut the wool blanket even with the raw edges of the quilt top. **(f)**

Pin both layers together around all edges and stitch with a 1.3cm (½in) seam allowance, leaving a 15cm (6in) opening for turning. Remove all the pins and clip the corners. **(g)**

Turn the throw right side out and carefully press the entire throw, turning under the seam allowance at the opening. Top-stitch 5mm (¼in) around all edges; this will close the opening as well as give a nice finished look. **(h)**

You now have a striking fairytale-of-a-throw blanket to keep you and yours warm.

VINTAGE

I admit to a bit of sentimentality, a slight propensity for nostalgia and a love of things vintage. I began my affair with vintage fabrics and linens at an early age – with lace doilies and hand-woven ticking inherited from my mother and her mother before. I thought of them all as treasure and sought them out wherever I could, from garage sales and second-hand stores. It took me some time before I could bring myself to cut into my treasures, but once I did I realized what a pleasure it was to re-create using the pieces I cherished, and how this act connected me to the past. Whether you have inherited or bought your vintage fabrics, find inspiration here to make some history of your own.

The Little Joy Dress is indeed a joy. This is one of my favourite projects – I love it for its simplicity; it's quick to whip up, and once you have your pattern you can make endless variations. I love it for the mix 'n' match vintage fabrics; playing with the combinations is all about "happy"! It works as a sweet summer dress, or something to wear over long-sleeve T-shirts and tights in cooler weather. Every dress is unique – just like the little girl it is made for.

YOU WILL NEED

Dress size shown: 4 years

- -

Approx. 1–2m (1–2 yards) of vintage fabrics in 4 different patterns (about 25cm/¼ yard each of 114cm/45in wide fabric), depending on dress size (see page 16)

- -

1.4m (1½ yards) bias binding, in two colours if preferred

- -

Vintage trims

- -

Vintage buttons

- -

Thread

 LEVEL

- -

INSTRUCTIONS

1. Cut the pattern pieces

Begin by preparing a simple A-line dress pattern in the appropriate size, as outlined on pages 17–18.

For this dress, I have used the standard pattern that is made up of 2 pieces: a front and back that are normally cut on the fold. Cut the pattern into 4 pieces and add the appropriate seam allowances (see page 18).

Now you have a front bodice pattern piece, a front skirt pattern piece, a back bodice piece, and a back skirt pattern piece. **(a)**

Transfer all the pattern markings to your fabric pieces and cut 2 of each piece (front bodice, front skirt, back bodice and back skirt) from 4 different fabrics, making sure that you flip each piece over to mark and cut a left and right side. **(b)**

2. Sew the front

Place the 2 front bodice pieces together, right sides facing, matching all raw edges, and pin along the centre seam allowance. **(c)**

Stitch the seam, back stitching at the beginning and end of your seams to secure the threads. Press. Finish all seams in your preferred method (see page 21).

Place the two front skirt pieces together, right sides facing, matching all raw edges, and pin along the centre seam allowance.

Stitch the seam, back-stitching at the beginning and end of your seams to secure the thread. Press.

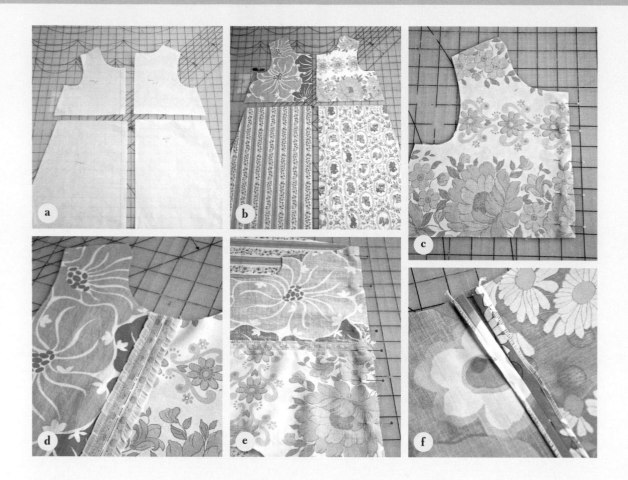

Attach vintage trim to the front bodice by pinning it in place along the centre seam and stitching to secure. **(d)**

Pin the bottom of the front bodice to the top of the front skirt with right sides together, matching the centre seams and raw edges. Machine stitch together and press the seam open. **(e)**

Attach a length of vintage trim along the seamline where the bodice and skirt meet, pinning it in place and then stitching to secure.

3. Sew the back
Pin together the two back bodice pieces, with right sides facing and raw edges aligned. Begin stitching the centre seam 9–10cm (3½–4in) below the neckline and continue stitching to the bottom.

Press the seam open, finish in your preferred method and top-stitch along both sides of the centre seam. **(f)**

Sew the back skirt pieces together in the same manner as the front. Then attach the back skirt to the back bodice as you did for the front of the dress. **(g)**

4. Sew the dress together
Place the front together with the back, right sides together, aligning the raw edges and pin at the shoulder seams and along the sides of the dress pieces. Stitch the shoulder and side seams, taking a 1cm (³/₈in) seam allowance. Press. **(h)**

Cut a length of bias binding long enough to fit around the neckline of the dress plus 50cm (20in). You need 25cm (10in) to overhang both ends of the back neck opening for a tie closure.

Measure 25cm (10in) of the length of bias binding and mark with a fabric marker or pin.

Begin attaching the bias binding from this mark to the neckline of the dress, starting at one side of the back neck opening.

Stitch the bias binding to the neckline (see page 14). You could use a decorative stitch if your sewing machine has this option. Stitch along the overhanging bias-binding fold to finish the ties. **(i)**

Attach bias binding to both armholes (see page 14). **(j)**

TIP
If you end up with slightly uneven ties, simply trim them to equal lengths and finish as normal.

5. Add the finishing touches
Hem the dress with a double hem by folding under 1cm (3/8in), then fold again by 1cm (3/8in), pin and stitch the hem. Press. **(k)**

For a sweet finishing touch, sew a couple of vintage buttons to the front centre bodice (see page 11).

This retro-inspired handbag is one of my favourite patterns. This is partly because it marked a turning point for me in my sewing – it was one of my first truly successful self-drafted, structured patterns – and partly because it really is the perfect handbag! It is just the right size to carry all the essentials, simple enough to make in a day, and a great pattern for the blossoming seamstress to challenge herself with. I've been keeping it all to myself, kind of like a little secret. It is high time that I share it.

I love making the Lola Handbag out of vintage fabrics. It also makes up beautifully in home-furnishing-weight fabric. It has such versatility – so many different looks that can be achieved just by your choice of fabrics. Have fun!

YOU WILL NEED

50 x 114cm (20 x 45in) outer fabric

50 x 114cm (20 x 45in) lining fabric

45cm (½ yard) medium-weight fusible interfacing

Button, approx. 2–3cm (¾–1in) diameter

18cm (7in) ribbon, 5–15mm (¼–½in) wide

Thread

LEVEL

TEMPLATES

Main panel, Side panel, Bottom panel, Handle, Interior pocket (see page 138)

NOTE

Due to the exact nature of the pattern, precise measurements are given

INSTRUCTIONS

1. Cut out the pattern pieces

Trace or copy the pattern pieces on page 138, making sure that you transfer all the markings from the pattern template to your pattern pieces. Cut the pieces from your fabric as follows: from the outer fabric: cut 2 main panels; 2 side panels; 1 bottom panel; 2 handles. From the lining: cut 2 main panels; 2 side panels; 1 bottom panel; 2 interior pockets. From the fusible interfacing: cut 2 main panels; 2 side panels; 1 bottom panel; 1 interior pocket. Transfer all markings on the pattern pieces to your fabric.

TIP

To achieve a crisper look on corner and side seams, trim the interfacing pieces 1.3cm (½in) from all edges. This removes any extra bulk from your seam allowance, creating a neater appearance.

Begin by fusing the fusible interfacing to the wrong side of the corresponding lining pieces, following the manufacturer's instructions.

2. Assemble the pocket

Take the 2 pocket pieces (one with interfacing) and place them with right sides facing with raw edges matching. Pin together. Stitch around all sides using a 1cm (³⁄₈in) seam

allowance, leaving a 5cm (2in) opening for turning, and back-stitching at the start and end of your seam to secure the thread. Clip the corners. **(a)**

Turn the pocket right side out, fold under the seam allowance at the opening, and press. Pin the pocket to the centre of one of the main lining panels. Top-stitch around the sides and bottom of the pocket close to the edge (this will close the opening used for turning), and make sure to back-stitch at the beginning and end of your stitching. Mark the centre of the pocket and stitch a line from top to bottom of the pocket to create compartments. **(b)**

For best results, press all of your seams as you go through your work – this will give your bag a nice, neat finish.

3. Sew the lining
Place one lining side panel right sides together with the main lining panel with the attached pocket, matching the raw edges, and pin in place. Using a fabric marker pen or pin, measure and mark 1.3cm (½in) up from bottom edge of the lining side panel. Stitch a 1.3cm (½in) seam from the top edge of the two pieces, stopping 1.3cm (½in) from the bottom (stop stitching at the mark on your fabric). Back-stitch to secure the thread. Repeat to attach the remaining side lining panel on the opposite edge. **(c)**

Now attach the remaining main lining panel by pinning it to one of the side lining panels, right sides together with raw edges matching. Stitch together using a 1.3cm (½in) seam allowance, again stopping at the mark on your fabric, or 1.3cm (½in) from the bottom edge. Repeat to sew the final seam.

Attach the bottom lining panel to one long edge of the main lining panels, with right sides together, matching the raw edges. Pin in place. Stitch the pieces together using a 1.3cm (½in) seam allowance: begin your line of stitching 1.3cm (½in) from the starting edge using the mark on your fabric as a guide, and end your stitching at the marking 1.3cm (½in) at the other end. Pin the short sides of the bottom lining panel to the side lining panels. Stitch together both sides, beginning and ending the seam following the markings on the pattern piece. **(d)**

Stitch the final long seam following the instructions for the first long seam, leaving a 10cm (4in) opening for turning. The lining is now complete. Turn the lining right side out. **(e)**

4. Sew the outer bag
Stitch the bag's exterior with the outer fabric pieces in the same way as the lining, without the pocket and without the opening in the bottom.

5. Sew the handles
Begin by pressing each handle piece in half lengthways, with wrong sides together, creating a centre crease. Open the handle piece and turn each long raw edge to meet at the centre crease. Press. Fold in half again and press. Top-stitch along all of the edges, about 5mm (¼in) from the edge all around. **(f)**

Pin the handles to either side of the main lining panels, placing each end of the handles 3.8cm (1½in) from the side seam, raw edges aligned, and tack in place close to the raw edge. Loop your ribbon, pin it to the centre of one of the main lining panels, and pin and tack in place. **(g)**

6. Finish the bag
Place the bag lining right side out, into the bag exterior wrong side out: the lining and the exterior should have right sides facing. Make sure that the handles and ribbon loop are safely tucked in and lying flat. Match the raw edges and seams, and pin in place. **(h)**

Stitch all the way around the top through both the exterior and lining, using a 1.3cm (½in) seam allowance, back-stitching at the start and end to secure the thread.

Turn your bag right side out using the opening in the lining. Once you have pulled everything through, stitch the opening closed either by hand using whip stitch or by machine. Tuck the bag lining into the inside of the bag, and smooth everything into place. Carefully press the top of the bag, then top-stitch around the edge.

Hand-stitch a vintage button to the main exterior panel, opposite the ribbon loop, making sure that it is positioned to ensure that the bag closes securely. **(i)** Hooray! Now it's time to take your new Lola Handbag out on the town!

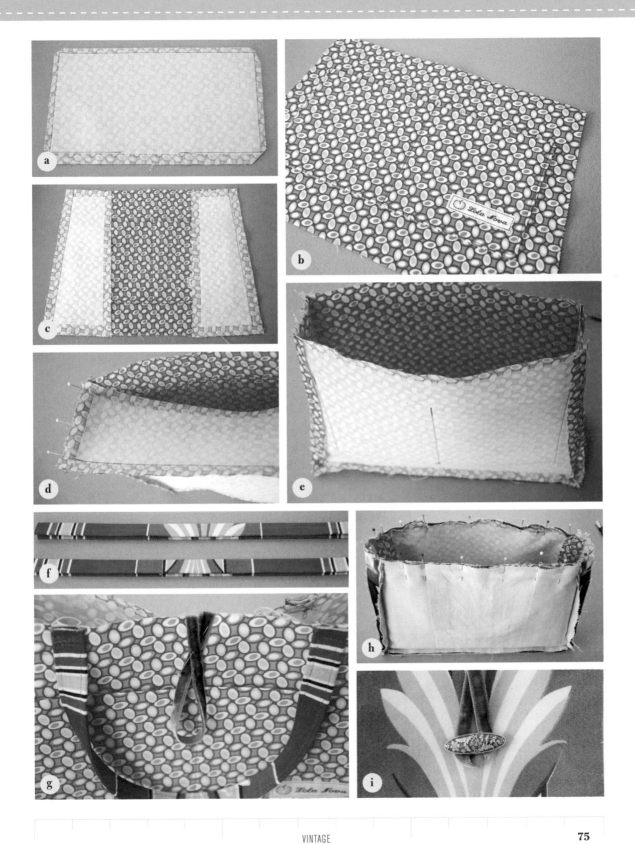

HOOK BOOK

I inherited a beautiful antique leather tri-fold hook-and-tool case from my grandmother; she, in turn, had inherited it from her mother. It is aged and worn with decades of use; full of tatting tools, crochet hooks, and needles of all shapes and sizes. It is a treasured heirloom that fills me with daydreams of all the beautiful things that were made using this case of precious items. After all these years, it has become too delicate for me to put to use, so I set out to make something reminiscent of it for my own tools, with a place for hooks and pen, a pocket for needles, stitch-markers and little snips, another pocket for notepaper or patterns, and a flap that keeps your tools from slipping out. Oh, but the Hook Book is very handy indeed, and not just for hooks! It makes a very nice picnic roll for cutlery, a clever device for make-up brushes and a pretty place for an artist's essentials.

YOU WILL NEED

Vintage fabric scraps, approx. four 25 x 43cm (10 x 17in) pieces and two 20 x 25cm (8 x 10in) pieces

Medium- to heavy-weight fusible interfacing

Vintage trims, doilies, lace for embellishment, if you wish

Buttons

Elastic cord

Thread

 ## LEVEL

NOTE

All seam allowances are 1cm (³⁄₈in) unless otherwise stated

INSTRUCTIONS

1. Prepare your fabric

Cut the following from vintage fabric: one 21 x 40cm (8¼ x 15¾in) lining rectangle (A); one 9 x 21cm (3½ x 8¼in) exterior rectangle (B); one 21 x 33.7cm (8¼ x 13¼in) exterior rectangle (C) in different fabric; two 12 x 40cm (4¾ x 15¾in) interior bottom pocket rectangles (D), one each in different fabrics; one 19 x 40cm (7½ x 15¾in) interior flap rectangle (E); one 13 x 15cm (5¼ x 6in) interior pocket flap (F).

Cut the following from the fusible interfacing: one 19 x 38cm (7½ x 15in) rectangle; one 7.5cm (3in) length of elastic cord.

Centre the rectangle of fusible interfacing on the wrong side of piece A and fuse together following the manufacturer's instructions. Set aside. **(a)**

2. Sew the exterior

Place pieces B and C together, with right sides facing and edges matching. Pin in place. Stitch together,

back-stitching at the beginning and end of the seam to secure the thread. Press and top-stitch close to the seam.

You can add any embellishments to the exterior at this stage and then set it aside. **(b)**

3. Sew the interior pockets and flap
Place the 2 pieces D right sides together, matching raw edges and pin along one long edge. **(c)** Stitch. Fold along the seam, wrong sides together, and press.

Fold interior flap piece E in half lengthways with right sides facing and matching raw edges. Stitch across both short ends using a 1.3cm (½in) seam allowance. Turn right side out and press. **(d)**

Fold piece F in half with right sides facing, short edges matching. Stitch across both short ends. Turn right side out and press. Top-stitch close to the edge around 3 sides of the flap. **(e)**

4. Sew the channels
Place bottom pocket D on the bottom edge of the right side of piece A, matching the raw edges. Pin in place. From the right edge of the lining piece measure in 13cm (5¼in) and draw a vertical line with a fabric-marker pen across the bottom pocket and lining piece. Do the same from the left edge, measuring in 13cm (5¼in), and mark a line. **(f)**

In the centre of these two lines, draw 4 more equally spaced vertical lines, approx. 2.5cm (1in) apart. Stitch along your drawn lines, over the pocket, making sure that you back-stitch at the beginning and end of stitching to secure the thread. **(g)**

5. Attach the interior pocket flap
Place pocket flap F approximately 2.5cm (1in) in from the left edge of the lining piece, about 5mm (¼in) above the pocket, with the raw edge facing towards the pocket and pin as shown. **(h)**

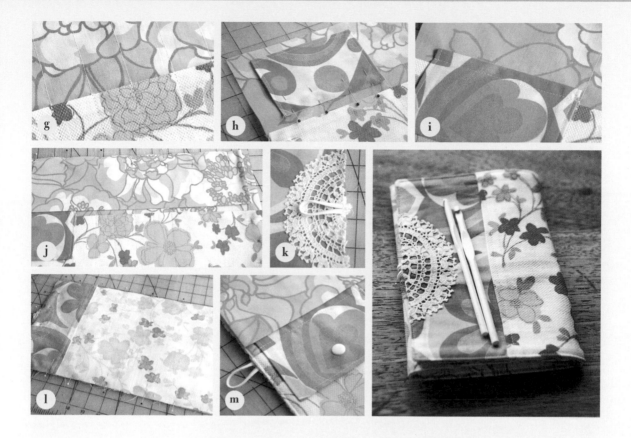

Stitch the flap in place, close to the raw edge. Fold the flap over towards the pocket, press it, and pin it in place. Top-stitch about 5mm (¼in) down from the top of the flap, making sure that you do not catch the top of the pocket in your stitching. **(i)**

Centre piece E along the top edge of the interior piece, matching raw edges, pin in place and tack close to the raw edge. **(j)**

TIP

To keep the interior flap, piece E, from getting caught in your stitching, fold back the corners and pin.

6. Assemble the Hook Book

Place the exterior piece of your Hook Book with the right side facing towards you. Fold the elastic cord into a loop and tack it to the centre of the short edge of the left side of the exterior piece, with the loop end pointing inwards, as shown. **(k)**

Place the exterior and interior pieces together, with right sides facing and matching all raw edges. Pin. Stitch around all of the edges, making sure to leave a 10cm (4in) opening for turning. **(l)**

Turn the Hook Book right side out and press carefully, folding under the opening seam allowance. Top-stitch very close to edges around all of the Hook Book sides.

Add a buttonhole to the interior pocket flap and hand-stitch a button to the pocket for a closure (see page 20), or you can use a snap fastener. **(m)**

Fold up your Hook Book into a tri-fold and using the elastic loop as a guide, mark the spot for a button. Hand-stitch your button at the mark.

All finished! Now you have a beautiful and useful Hook Book to carry your tools, and perhaps pass down to future generations, or give as a wonderfully useful gift.

The laundry is always there for you. At least that is how it is at my house; why not make it a more pleasant sight by whipping up a pretty vintage-inspired laundry bag? Using vintage fabrics and trims gives these functional pieces a rather romantic feel. I have created a large bag for the basics and a small one for delicates.

If you want to know a little secret, these bags have a myriad of uses beyond storing laundry. I have made them up in fun, child-friendly prints and hung them on hooks. The small size becomes the perfect tidy for all those little toys, blocks and game pieces that seem to defy normal storage. Easy to open and close, even the smallest people in your home can pour out the loot for play, and then know exactly where to put them away again. The large bag makes for great dressing-up clothes storage. I could go on with 101 ways to use these bags, but I've no doubt you can come up some very clever ideas by yourself!

 YOU WILL NEED

For the small laundry bag:

50 x 76–114cm (20 x 30–45in) vintage print fabric

50 x 76–114cm (20 x 30–45in) co-ordinating vintage print fabric

1m (1 yard) vintage lace trim or ribbon, any width

2m (2 yards) ribbon or twill tape, 13mm (½in) wide

Small scrap of fusible interfacing, approx. 2.5–3.8cm (1–1½in) square

Thread

For the large laundry bag:

1m x 76–114cm (1 yard x 30–45in) vintage print fabric

1m x 76–114cm (1 yard x 30–45in) co-ordinating vintage print fabric

1.5m (1½ yards) vintage lace trim or ribbon, any width

2m (2 yards) ribbon or twill tape, 13mm (½in) wide

Small scrap of fusible interfacing, approx. 2.5–3.8cm (1–1½in) square

Thread

 LEVEL

 NOTES

All seam allowances are 13mm (½in) unless otherwise stated. Instructions are the same for both the small and large bags.

 INSTRUCTIONS

1. Prepare your fabrics

For the small laundry bag: Cut two 35.5 x 39cm (14 x 15½in) rectangles from main print fabric. Cut two 18 x 35.5cm (7 x 14in) rectangles from co-ordinating fabric. Cut two 35.5cm (14in) lengths of lace or ribbon.

For the large laundry bag: Cut two 49.5 x 51cm (19½ x 20in) rectangles from main print fabric. Cut two 25 x 51cm (10 x 20in) rectangles from co-ordinating fabric. Cut two 51cm (20in) lengths of lace or ribbon.

2. Sew the panels

Place one of the smaller rectangles on the bottom of the larger rectangle, right sides together and raw edges matching. Pin along the seam allowance, as shown. **(a)**

Stitch along the pinned edge and press. Finish the seam allowances in your preferred method (see page 21). Repeat the process for the remaining rectangles.

Place one length of lace or ribbon along the seam line of one of your sewn rectangles and pin in place. Stitch the

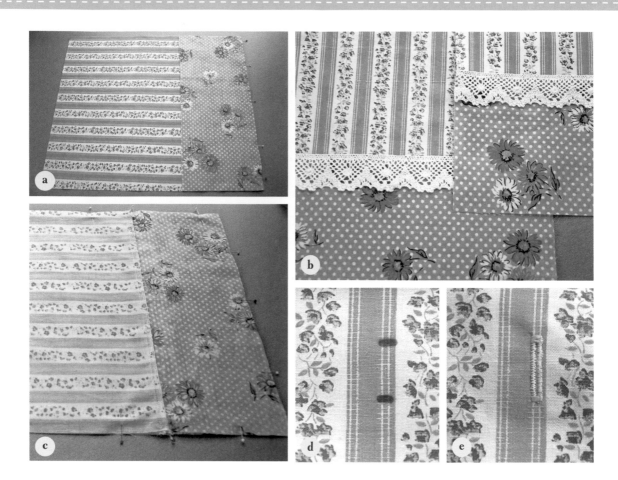

lace or ribbon to the panel using a straight stitch. Repeat this process for the remaining panel. **(b)**

3. Assemble the bag

Place one panel on top of the other panel, right sides facing and matching raw edges. Pin in place along the bottom and 2 long sides. **(c)**

Stitch around the 3 pinned sides, back-stitching at the beginning and end of your seams. Finish your seam allowances in your preferred method.

4. Sew the buttonhole

Turn the laundry bag right side out. With a fabric marker, make a mark 12cm (4¾in) from the top edge in the centre of one panel. Make a second mark above the first 10cm (4in) from the top edge of the bag, as shown. This marks the placement of your buttonhole. **(d)**

On the wrong side of the laundry bag, fuse a small piece of interfacing over the markings you have just made; this adds stability to your buttonhole.

Working from the right side of the laundry bag, use the buttonhole setting on your machine (refer to your sewing machine manual as machines can differ greatly) to begin stitching the buttonhole at the top 10cm (4in) mark, end the buttonhole at the bottom 12cm (4¾in) mark. Cut open the buttonhole. **(e)**

5. Sew the drawstring casing

Turn the laundry bag to the wrong side. Fold over 2.5cm (1in) at the top edge and press. Fold the top edge over again by 5cm (2in) and press. **(f)**

Pin the folded edge in place and stitch 2.5cm (1in) from the top edge of the bag around the entire edge, making

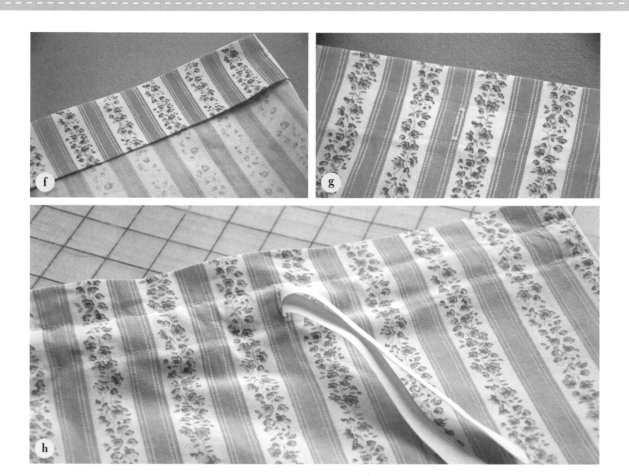

sure not to stitch across the buttonhole. Sew another line of stitching just below the bottom of the buttonhole, approx. 5cm (2in) from the top edge of the laundry bag, again making sure that you do not stitch over the buttonhole. This creates the casing for the drawstring. **(g)**

Turn the bag right side out. Attach one end of ribbon or twill tape to a bodkin or safety pin and push it into the casing at the buttonhole. Keep feeding it through the channel until it reappears at the other end. Pull the ribbon or twill tape through, then remove the bodkin or safety pin. With the top of the bag fully open, you want to have at least 13–15cm (5–6in) of both ends of the ribbon or twill tape extending. **(h)**

I recommend tying both ends together in a knot to keep the ends from slipping up into the casing. Pull on the knotted ends of the ribbon to draw the bag closed.

IN DREAMS FABRIC HEADBOARD

Anyone who knows me knows that I love to change things around in the Little Green Cottage. At least once a season you can find me rearranging the furniture, shuffling bits about, and generally altering the look of things.

The In Dreams Fabric Headboard came to me while I was dreaming up a new look for my bed – I am so often inspired by vintage fabrics in my décor. Buying a whole new piece of furniture was a bit impractical, but this project matched my desire for a change of scene perfectly. The headboard is simply hung from a curtain pole attached to the wall above your bed. It is reversible, so you get two looks in one! The headboard will fit a double bed; however, you can increase and decrease the number of panels to fit different bed widths. I think it would be a charming project for a child's room, too.

YOU WILL NEED

2 patterned vintage pillowcases

1 patterned vintage sheet (any size)

1 white or light-coloured plain sheet, or 2m (2 yards) muslin or white fabric

9 buttons

Selection of vintage embellishments, such as doilies, lace, ribbons and embroidery

Light-weight fusible interfacing

Thread

LEVEL

NOTE

All seam allowances are 1cm (³/₈in) unless otherwise stated

INSTRUCTIONS

1. Prepare the pillowcases
Begin by pressing the two pillowcases with a hot iron, making sure that you straighten the seams.

Cut each of the pillowcases into 2 rectangle panels: lay the pillowcase flat on your cutting surface and carefully cut up the side seam. **(a)**

Continue to cut along the top or end seam, creating one large flat piece of fabric. Next, cut along the side fold to create 2 panels from one case. Repeat for the second pillowcase. Put one of the panels aside so that you are left with 3 panels.

Use a rotary cutter or shears to straighten the edges and trim the panels to equal measurements.

2. Sew and embellish the panels
Place the long edge of one panel on top of another, right sides facing and matching raw edges and hems. (The hemmed edge of the pillowcases will be the bottom of your headboard.) Pin in place.

Stitch along the pinned edge, taking a 1cm (³/₈in) seam allowance and back-stitching at the beginning and end of your line of stitching. Stitch the remaining panel to the first two in the same way. Press the seams.

Once the panels have been sewn and pressed, take the measurements of the completed piece. Using these measurements, cut one large rectangle from the vintage sheet – this will be the reverse side of your headboard. Cut one large rectangle from the plain sheet to the same measurements – this will be the inner lining.

Arrange your embellishments on the pieced panel section, pin them in place and stitch. **(b)**

Now embellish the reverse side rectangle, if you wish.

3. Make the tabs
Attach a large piece of fusible interfacing to your lining fabric before cutting it into strips. This saves time and effort! Cut nine 7.5 x 25.5cm (3 x 10in) strips of fabric from the remaining pillowcase panel for the tab

---

exterior. Cut nine 7.5 x 25.5cm (3 x 10in) strips from the remaining vintage sheet fabric for the tab lining.

Pin the exterior and lining strips together with right sides facing and raw edges matching. Stitch around 3 sides with a 5mm (¼in) seam allowance, leaving one short end unstitched. Turn right side out and press. Top-stitch 5mm (¼in) from the stitched edges around the three edges.

Starting at 2.5cm (1in) from the stitched end of each tab, stitch a buttonhole to fit the size of buttons you have chosen (see page 20). **(c)**

With the tabs' lining side facing the right side of the headboard front, pin the tabs along the top of the

headboard panel with raw edges matching. Position the tabs at each end, 1.3cm (½in) from the short sides, and evenly space the remaining tabs along the top edge, pinning in place. **(d)**

Tack the tabs in place, 5mm (¼in) from the top edge. Pin the loose ends of the tabs to the front panel to keep them from shifting during the remainder of your sewing.

4. Sew the headboard
Place the reverse panel on top of your headboard front panel with right sides facing, matching the raw edges. **(e)**

Place the inner lining panel on top of the reverse panel, again matching the raw edges. Pin all the layers in place.

Stitch all the way around using a 1cm (⅜in) seam allowance, leaving a 15cm (6in) opening for turning. Back-stitch at the beginning and end of your stitching.

Turn the headboard piece right side out and remove the pins from the tabs. Turn under the seam allowance at the opening and carefully press the entire headboard. Top-stitch 5mm (¼in) from all the edges, this will close the opening.

Using a water-soluble fabric marker, mark the position for all of the buttons on the front panel. **(f)**

Sew the buttons to the front at the marked points (see page 20). **(g) (h)**

Now simply hang your In Dreams Fabric Headboard from an attached curtain rod above your bed! Sweet dreams!

TIP
You can easily increase the size to complement a larger bed: simply add another pillowcase panel and stitch 3 extra tabs. For a twin/single, or child's bed, use 2 panels and 7 tabs.

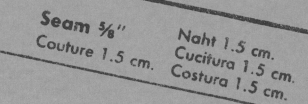

Seam ⅝"
Couture 1.5 cm.

Naht 1.5 cm.
Cucitura 1.5 cm.
Costura 1.5 cm.

ECLECTIC

Eclectic is usually the first word I think of when
it comes to describing my style. I like to mix it
up a bit, putting unexpected elements together:
a little romance with my industrial, a little
kitsch with my classical, a little frivolous with
my utilitarian. Eclectic need not be cluttered
or fussy; I enjoy a clean line and some function
with my form. I like things that tell a story.
For the projects in this chapter I wanted to
create items that were useful, a little modern
and slightly quirky. These projects are easily
adaptable to your own personal style,
and I hope that you will be inspired to make
things that tell the story of you.

Place on Straight Grain of Fabric

Placez sur le droit fil
Im geraden Fadenlauf auflegen
Sistemare sul dritto filo del tessuto
Colocar al hilo de la tela

"CALL ME" CUSHION COVER

The "Call Me" Cushion Cover is a quirky project that is the perfect conversation starter. Done up in graphic prints and blocks of bold colour, it stands out from the crowd. The imagery is created using stencils with fabric paint and a little stitching.

YOU WILL NEED

50 x 114cm (20 x 45in) cotton print fabric

Various cotton scraps: approx. 12.5 x 50cm (5 x 20in) dark fabric; 23 x 23cm (9 x 9in) light fabric; 23 x 23cm (9 x 9in) contrasting cotton print fabric

Fabric marker

Trims for embellishment (optional)

Freezer-paper

Black paint

Foam brush

Thread

40cm (16in) square cushion pad

LEVEL

TEMPLATES

Telephone, Telephone poles (see page 136)

INSTRUCTIONS

1. Prepare the fabric and stencils

For the back cushion panels: cut two rectangles, 33 x 44.5cm (13 x 17.5in), from the cotton print. For the front cushion pieces: cut one 24 x 44.5cm (9.5 x 17.5in) rectangle from the cotton print; one 7.5 x 44.5cm (3 x 17.5in) strip from dark fabric; one 18 x 18cm (7 x 7in) square from light fabric; two 16 x 18cm (6¼ x 7in) rectangles from a contrasting cotton print.

Prepare the stencils from the templates on page 136, following the techniques on page 13. Stencil the telephone poles onto the cotton print rectangle for the front.

Stencil the telephone symbol on the light fabric square. Leave to dry and set the paint according to the manufacturer's instructions. **(a)**

2. Sew the details

Take the rectangle with the telephone-pole stencil and, using a fabric marker, draw some telephone wires along the tops of the poles as shown. **(b)**

Stitch along the lines you have drawn with black thread, remove the fabric marker lines and set aside.

3. Sew the cushion front

Gather the square with the telephone symbol print and the 2 smaller, contrasting cotton print rectangles.

Place one cotton print rectangle on the telephone symbol print square with right sides facing, matching raw edges, and pin in place.

Stitch along the pinned edge using a 1.5cm (⅝in) seam allowance. Stitch the remaining cotton print rectangle to the opposite side. **(c)**

Place the dark fabric strip together with the pieces you have just sewn, right sides facing and raw edges matching. Pin. Stitch together using a 1.5cm (⅝in) seam allowance. **(d)**

Add any embellishments to your pieces at this point.

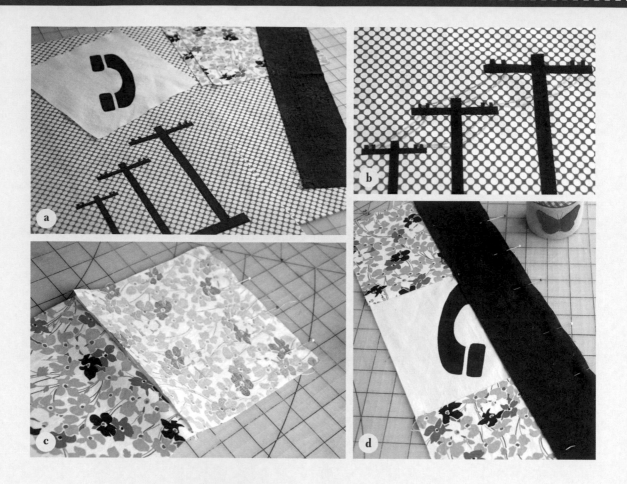

Place the dark fabric strip edge with the large telephone pole rectangle piece, right sides facing and with matching edges. Pin and stitch with a 1.5cm (⅝in) seam allowance. Press all seams. **(e)**

4. Sew the back panels

Fold over 2.5cm (1in) along one long edge of the rectangle, with the wrong sides together, and press. Fold over 2.5cm (1in) again, press and pin in place. Stitch close to the pinned edge. Repeat this process for the remaining rectangle. **(f)**

5. Assemble the cushion cover

Lay the cushion-cover front out flat on your work surface with the right side facing up. Place one of the back panels over the front piece, right sides together and raw edges matching. Pin around the outer edges.

Place the remaining back panel on the opposite side, so that the sewn edges overlap in the centre. **(g)**

Stitch around all of the edges using a 1.5cm (⅝in) seam allowance. Turn the cushion cover right side out through the back opening, and press.

Just tuck in a cushion pad and your "Call Me" Cushion Cover is ready to be admired!

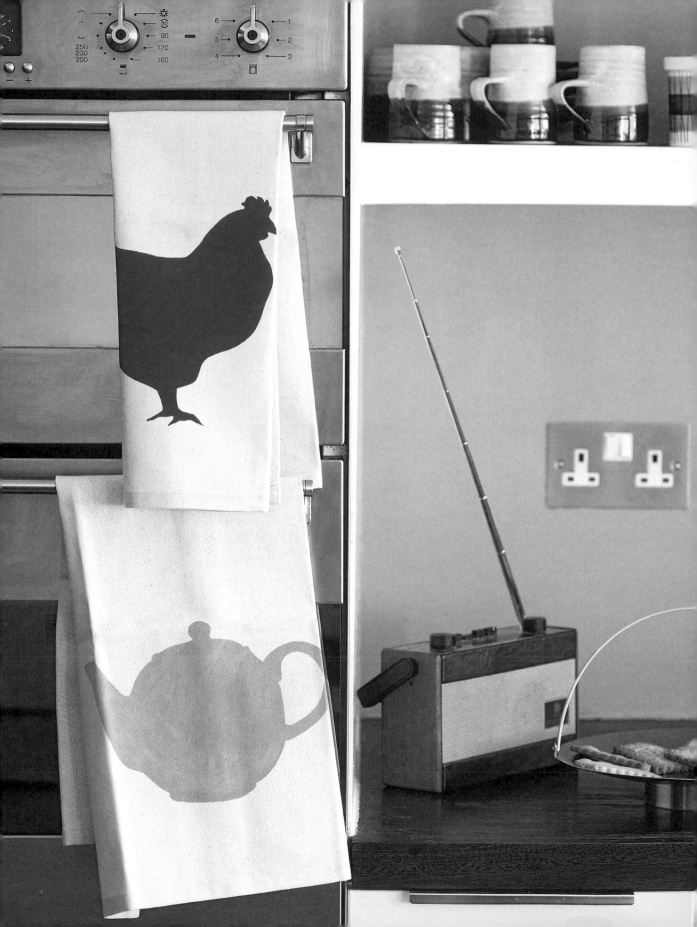

Who doesn't love a great tea towel? These tea towels are quite simple to make, they are so useful, and add a pop of colour as well as a little adventure to your kitchen. They make gorgeous house-warming, hostess or wedding gifts.

This project is the perfect introduction to freezer-paper stencils. You can use the templates provided, or go wild and come up with your own unique designs. Use typographic rubber stamps and fabric paint for personalized lettering. Once you make one you'll want to make more – a lot more!

YOU WILL NEED

50 x 114cm (20 x 45in) white or cream fabric (choose a medium-weight fabric that is either 100% cotton, 100% linen or a cotton–linen blend)

13cm (5in) white or cream twill tape, 13mm (½in) wide

Pencil

Freezer paper

Fabric paint

Foam brush

Thread

LEVEL

 TEMPLATES

Cup, Teapot, Chicken (see page 139)

INSTRUCTIONS

1. Prepare your fabric
From your fabric cut a 43 x 74cm (17 x 29in) rectangle. Double hem all edges of the rectangle by folding each raw edge over by 1cm (³⁄₈in), then folding again by 1cm (³⁄₈in). Pin in place. **(a)**

Cut a length of twill tape to fit across one corner of the tea towel, pin the twill tape under the folded hem, as shown overleaf. **(b)**

Sew the hem around all sides, stitching close to the inner folded edge.

2. Stencil your tea towel
Copy the templates on page 139 and prepare your freezer-paper stencil as described on page 13. When cutting out the teapot and cup stencils, make sure that you preserve the handle cut-outs, as shown. **(c)**

For this example, I placed the teapot stencil at one end of the towel, and the tea cup stencil at the other end, but you can place them however takes your fancy. Once you have chosen your stencil placement, iron the stencil (see page

13), making sure that you have placed the handle cut-out part of the stencils in the correct position, as shown. **(d)**

Apply the fabric paint evenly with the foam brush for both stencils. Let the paint dry, then remove the stencil. Set the fabric paint according to the manufacturer's instructions. **(e)**

You are now are the proud owner of a magnificent Tea Towel of Distinction!

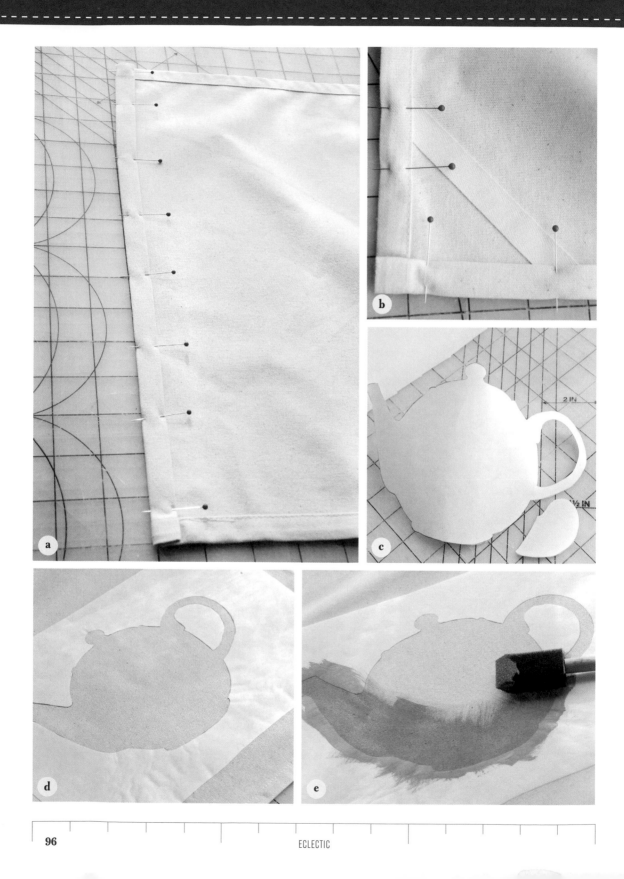

A zipped pouch for the artist. Whether your tools be pencils, pens, paintbrushes, make-up, crochet hooks or other, this is the perfect carrying case. The measurements can easily be adjusted to suit your particular needs. These make excellent gifts for students, friends and teachers... well, just about anyone, really.

The Artist's Pouch makes perfect use of fabric scraps left over from other projects, or could be made from re-use materials.

YOU WILL NEED

A combination of fabric scraps, including approx. 35.5 x 35.5cm (14 x 14in) of exterior fabric and approx. 38 x 40cm (15 x 16in) fabric for lining

- -

Embellishments – I used rubber stamps and fabric paint, but you could add ribbons, buttons, lace and suchlike

- -

23cm (9in) zip

- -

Masking tape

- -

Light- or medium-weight fusible interfacing

- -

21cm (8in) length of ribbon, 15mm (⅝in) wide

- -

Thread

- -

Seam ripper

- -

Tea towel, for pressing

 LEVEL

- -

 ## INSTRUCTIONS

1. Prepare your fabrics
Cut two 13 x 28cm (5 x 11in) rectangles from each of the following: exterior fabric, lining fabric and fusible interfacing. Cut two 4 x 10.5cm (1½ x 4in) rectangles from lining fabric. Cut two 10.5cm (4in) lengths of ribbon.

Embellish the two plain exterior fabric pieces, if you desire. I used rubber stamps and fabric paint (see page 12). Set aside. **(a)**

2. Prepare the pouch
After you have cut all of your pieces, fuse the interfacing to the 2 larger lining pieces on the wrong sides.

Take the 2 small lining pieces and fold them in half, wrong sides together, short ends matching, and press to create a centre line. Fold over each short end 1.5cm (⅝in) towards the centre crease. Press and set aside. These will be used for attaching the zip. **(b)**

Take the 2 interfaced lining pieces and place together with right sides facing, matching raw edges, and pin in place along one long edge. Tack together using a 1.5cm (⅝in) seam allowance. Press the seam allowance open. **(c)**

Take the 2 exterior fabric pieces. Fold over 1.3cm (½in) along one long edge, wrong sides together, and press. Repeat for the second piece.

3. Attach the zip
Sandwich each end of your zip between the folds of the lining pieces prepared earlier in step 2, with the creased end facing outward. Pin in place.

For a better finish, open the zip a few centimetres on one end, bring the zipper teeth together and use a small piece of masking tape to hold it in place. Sandwich the zipper end in the folded fabric and pin. **(d)**

Stitch across the ends close to the edge of the fabric, back-stitching at the beginning and end of your stitches. Close the zip. **(e)**

Lay the wrong side of the zip on the wrong side of your lining pieces, making sure to centre the zip along the tacked seam in the lining. Pin in place.

Place the folded edge of one of your exterior pieces along one side of the zip close to the teeth, with wrong side facing the wrong side of your lining, matching raw edges, and pin in place. Stitch close to the zip using a zipper foot on your sewing machine. **(f)**

Repeat the process on the opposite side of the zipper for the remaining exterior piece.

4. Assemble the pouch

The folded pieces of lining fabric sewn to the ends of the zip will extend a little beyond the raw edges of the lining and exterior pieces. Trim them so that they are flush with the raw edges. **(g)**

Unzip the zip partially and, using a seam ripper, remove the tacking stitches on the lining seam.

Fold the exterior pieces together right sides facing, matching raw edges, and pin along the long edge. Do the same for the lining pieces. **(h)**

Stitch the exterior pieces together using a 1.3cm (½in) seam allowance. Repeat for the lining pieces, making sure to leave a 7.5cm (3in) opening for turning.

5. Finish the pouch

Prepare your two lengths of ribbon by folding them in half. Now fold your sewn pieces so that the zipper, exterior seam and lining seam are centred on top of each other and in the middle as shown. Again, be sure that you have opened your zip, otherwise you will not be able to turn the pouch right side out. **(i)**

Place one folded length of ribbon at either end, in between the layers of your exterior fabric, with the fold facing inside, raw edges matching, centred over the zip. Pin in place as shown. **(j)**

Pin all the layers together at the short ends. Stitch through all of the layers using a 1.5cm (⅝in) seam allowance, back-stitching at the beginning and end of your seam. Clip the corners. **(k)**

Turn the pouch right side out with the lining on the outside. Stitch the opening closed with your preferred method.

6. Make the boxed corners

Pinch each corner into a triangle with the seam running down the centre. Feel to make sure that no extra fabric is folded into your triangle; you want it as smooth as possible. Pin your triangles. **(l)**

Make a mark with a fabric marker 1.3cm (½in) from the tip of your triangle at the centre seam. Stitch a line perpendicular to the seam at this mark. Repeat for the remaining corners. **(m)**

Turn the pouch right side out and press. Place a rolled-up tea towel inside the pouch to assist in pressing.

Voilà! You now have a work of art to house your art tools!

TIP

If you want a custom-sized pouch for a certain tool, such as a paintbrush or pair of knitting needles, just increase the length of your main rectangles (exterior and lining). Keep in mind that as you increase the length you will also need to choose a longer zip.

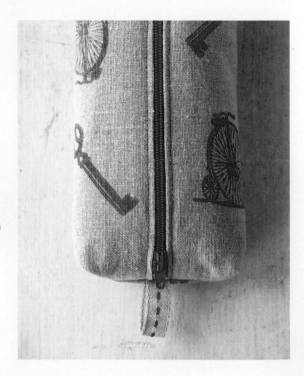

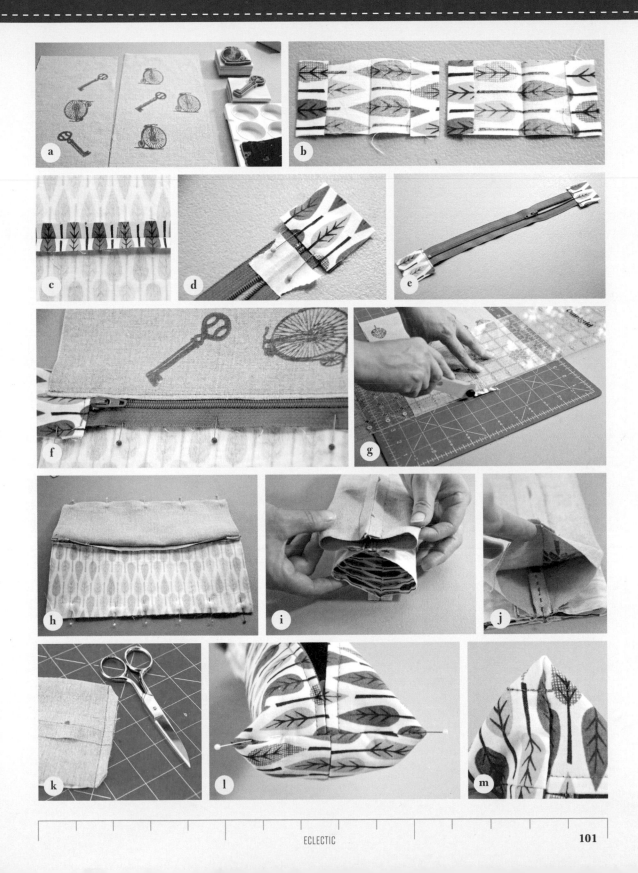

I do so like to have a place for everything, even if at times not everything is in its place. These Everything Baskets, in two sizes, have become essentials in the Little Green Cottage. They have found homes in the kitchen for tea, garlic, gadgets and much more. There are several making an appearance in my creative space, holding just about anything you can think of. Good for the bathroom, the kids' rooms, the games cupboard; these baskets are so useful and look so lovely!

This pattern is incredibly versatile; the baskets can be made up in felt as well as cotton, linen, corduroy and wool.

YOU WILL NEED

For each basket:

Two 30.5 x 46cm (12 x 18in) sheets of felt (in two different colours)

One 23 x 30.5cm (9 x 12in) sheet of felt in a third colour

Heavy-weight fusible interfacing

25cm (10in) length of ribbon, 13–25mm (½–1in) wide

Thread

Button or other embellishment (optional)

● ● LEVEL

● NOTE

All seam allowances are 1cm (⅜in) unless otherwise stated. The instructions have been written for the large size basket with any differences for the small basket noted in square brackets [ ].

INSTRUCTIONS

1. Prepare your fabric
For the large basket:
For the exterior: cut one 30.5 x 30.5cm (12 x 12in) square from one colour of felt; two 7.5 x 30.5cm (3 x 12in) strips from the smaller sheet of felt. For the lining: cut one 30.5 x 41cm (12 x 16¼in) rectangle from one sheet of felt; one 30.5 x 38cm (12 x 15in) rectangle of fusible interfacing.

For the small basket:
For the exterior: cut one 20 x 25cm (8 x 10in) rectangle from one colour of felt; two 7.5 x 25cm (3 x 10in) strips from the smaller sheet of felt. For the lining: cut one 25 x 31cm (10 x 12¼in) rectangle from one sheet of felt; one 25 x 28cm (10 x 11in) rectangle of fusible interfacing.

2. Sew the sides
Pin each of the two 7.5 x 30.5cm (3 x 12in) [7.5 x 25cm (3 x 10in)] felt strips on either side of the 30.5 x 30.5cm (12 x 12in) [20 x 25cm (8 x 10in)] felt rectangle, matching edges. **(a)**

Stitch along the pinned allowance, back-stitching at the beginning and end of your seam. Press the seams open and top-stitch close to both seams, as shown. **(b)**

Fold the sewn felt piece in half, right sides together, edges matching with the strips of felt at the top. Pin both sides of the folded piece, as shown. **(c)**

Stitch along both pinned sides, back-stitching at the beginning and end. Clip the bottom corners of the seam allowance on both sides and press the seams open. **(d)**

3. Make the boxed corners
To make the boxed corners, pull the bottom corner of the seam and pinch into a triangle, making sure to centre the seam. You may choose to place a pin into the triangle to keep it from shifting as you work.

Next, using a seam gauge or ruler, measure 7.5cm (3in) [5cm (2in)] from the tip of the triangle and make a mark with a fabric marker in the centre of the seam.

Using your ruler, draw a straight line across at the 7.5cm (3in) [5cm (2in)] mark, as shown. **(e)**

Repeat this process for the remaining corner. **(f)**

Stitch along the lines that you have just drawn, back-stitching at the beginning and end of your seams. Trim away the excess triangle, making sure not to cut through your stitches. **(g)**

Fold over 13mm (½in) at the top of the basket and press. **(h)**

Turn the basket right side out.

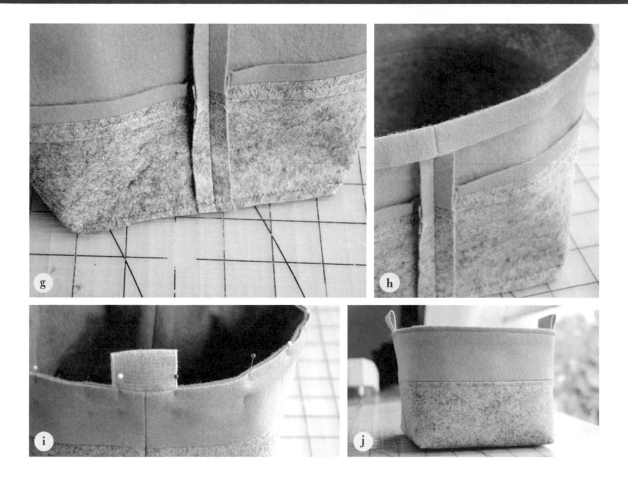

4. Sew the lining

To make the lining, centre the fusible interfacing on the largest felt rectangle and fuse in place following the manufacturer's instructions.

Fold the interfaced rectangle in half across the width, right sides together, and continue to follow the steps for the exterior from the text after illustration (b) until the text just before illustration (h). Leave the lining wrong side out.

5. Finish the basket

Tuck the basket lining inside the basket exterior, matching side seams and the top edge. Cut two 11.5cm (4½in) lengths of ribbon and fold them in half. Tuck the raw edges of the ribbon in between the exterior and lining at the side seams and pin in place. Pin the lining and exterior together around the entire top edge of the basket. **(i)**

Top-stitch approx. 5mm (¼in) from the top edge around the entire basket; this will secure the ribbon handles. **(j)**

Add a hand-sewn button or other embellishment to your basket, if you so desire.

URBAN ORGANIZER

Urban Organizer has a nice ring to it, don't you think? Many of us hope to be more organized – urban or not, we could all use more storage. A place for incoming and outgoing mail, a spot for the latest magazine we haven't yet had a moment to savour, somewhere where the elusive TV remote, keys and reading glasses can all be tucked away and quickly found in handy pockets. Oh, I do love a handy pocket!

This unique catch-all is really a sturdy curtain, easily hung from a rod that is either attached to a wall or door for optimal use of space. How handy to have a place for all these things, and one that takes up such a small amount of space itself.

TIP

This project could easily be modified for use as an art supply caddy, a homework station, and a craft centre… there are so many possibilities!

YOU WILL NEED

2m x 114cm (2 yards x 45in) home-furnishing-weight fabric (I used unbleached cotton twill), for the main curtain

2m x 114cm (2 yards x 45in) lining fabric (I used unbleached cotton muslin)

1m x 114cm (1 yard x 45in) print home-furnishing-weight fabric (I used a red and natural ticking stripe), for the pockets

1.5m (1½ yards) strapping or webbing that is 2.5–5cm (1–2in) wide

Medium-weight fusible interfacing

Thread

Various trims, ribbons and buttons for embellishment (these are optional)

LEVEL

NOTE

All seam allowances are 1cm (³/₈in) unless otherwise stated

INSTRUCTIONS

1. Prepare your fabric

For the main curtain: cut one 66 x 129.5cm (26 x 51in) rectangle from the main fabric and one 66 x 129.5cm (26 x 51in) rectangle from the lining fabric.

For the print pockets: cut two 18 x 30.5cm (7 x 12in) rectangles; two 24 x 30.5cm (9½ x 12in) rectangles; two 28 x 30.5cm (11 x 12in) rectangles from the print fabric.

For the small pockets: cut four 15 x 18cm (6 x 7in) rectangles from the main fabric.

For the pocket linings: cut two 18 x 30.5cm (7 x 12in) rectangles; two 24 x 30.5cm (9½ x 12in) rectangles; two 28 x 30.5cm (11 x 12in) rectangles; four 15 x 18cm (6 x 7in) rectangles from the lining fabric.

From the interfacing: cut two 18 x 30.5cm (7 x 12in) rectangles; two 24 x 30.5cm (9½ x 12in)

two 28 x 30.5cm (11 x 12in) rectangles; four 15 x 18cm (6 x 7in) rectangles.

From the webbing: cut five 25.5cm (10in) lengths.

Begin by fusing the interfacing to the corresponding pocket lining pieces following the manufacturer's instructions, then set them aside.

2. Sew the main curtain

Fold the webbing lengths in half. Pin the ends of one folded length of webbing to the right side of your main fabric rectangle along the top edge, placing it 2.5cm (1in) in from the side edge, matching raw edges, with the fold facing inward. Pin a second folded length of webbing 2.5cm (1in) in from the opposite side edge. Pin the remaining 3 folded webbing lengths evenly spaced along the top edge. Tack the webbing in place. **(a)**

Place the lining rectangle on top of the main rectangle, right sides facing and matching raw edges. Pin and then stitch all 4 sides, making sure to leave a 15cm (6in) opening for turning.

Turn right side out, fold under the seam allowance at the opening and press. Top-stitch along the top and bottom edge, this will close the opening. I used a decorative stitch on my machine for the bottom edge to add interest; however you can use a simple straight stitch if you prefer. **(b)**

3. Prepare the pockets

If you wish to add embellishment to your pockets, do so at this stage by attaching ribbon or buttons, or using decorative stitches on the front of your pocket pieces.

All of the pockets are sewn using the same method: place each pocket front piece with a corresponding interfaced lining pocket piece, right sides facing and raw edges matching, and pin along the seam allowances on all sides.

Stitch the seam, leaving a 7.5cm (3in) opening at the top edge of your pocket for turning. Clip the corners of the sewn pocket. **(c)**

Turn the pocket right side out. Fold under the seam allowance at the opening and press carefully. To finish the pocket, top-stitch along the top edge only, this will close the opening. **(d)**

Repeat this process for the remaining pockets.

4. Attach the pockets

Take your two 15 x 28cm (6 x 11in) finished pockets; these will be the top pockets of your organizer. Place one of the pockets 13cm (5in) down from the top edge and 2.5cm (1in) in from the left-hand side and pin in place. Repeat for the second pocket on the right-hand side of the organizer, leaving a gap of approx. 2.5cm (1in) between the two pockets. **(e)**

Stitch the pockets in place close to the pocket edges around the sides and bottom edge of the pocket, back-stitching at the beginning and end of your stitching. **(f)**

Next, take the four 13 x 15cm (5 x 6in) finished pockets; these will be your second row of pockets on the organizer.

Place one of the pockets 10cm (4in) down from the bottom edge of the top pockets and 2.5cm (1in) in from the left-hand side of the organizer. Pin in place. Repeat for a second pocket on the right-hand side. Place the remaining two small pockets evenly spaced between the outer two pockets, leaving a gap of approx. 2.5cm (1in) between all the pockets. Stitch the pockets to the organizer. **(g)**

Take the two 21.5 x 28cm (8½ x 11in) finished pockets; these will be your third row of pockets.

Place one of the pockets 10cm (4in) down from the bottom edge of the previous row of pockets and 2.5cm (1in) in from the left-hand side. Pin in place. Repeat for the second pocket on the right-hand side of the organizer. Stitch the pockets to the organizer.

Finally, take the two 25.5 x 28cm (10 x 11in) finished pockets for the bottom row. Place one of the pockets 10cm (4in) down from the bottom edge of the previous row of pockets and 2.5cm (1in) in from the left-hand side of the organizer. Pin in place. Repeat for the second pocket on the right-hand side. Stitch the pockets to the organizer. **(h)**

The Urban Organizer is now ready to be hung in the same fashion as a tab top curtain from a rod attached to the wall or door. You will want to make sure it is fairly sturdy and secure to take the weight of your stored items.

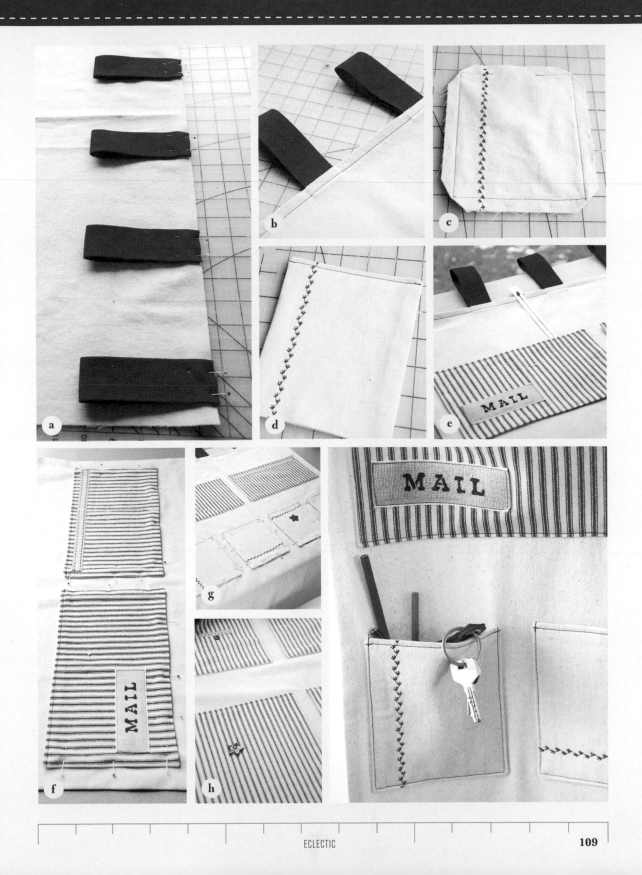

WHIMSY

Once, when I was young, a family friend gave
me a present that was small enough to fit in
the palm of my hand. It was colourful, a funny
shape and had a smooth feel. I had no idea what
it was, but it made me smile. When I asked what
it could be the friend said to me, "It is a whimsy,
it can be anything you might imagine".
Whimsy is such a wonderful little word.
It means "playfully quaint or fanciful
behaviour, a fanciful or fantastic device, object
or creation", which I think perfectly fits the
projects in this chapter. They make me happy,
make me feel a little silly and childlike, and
I think we can all do with some of that in our
lives. Many of these projects are scrappy ones,
perfect for using up happy bits of this and that.
These are creations to give you a smile –
simply good things to make.

"Deer Diary, let me tell you a secret…"

I love a brand-new diary or journal, with all the promise and possibility of a fresh start. This sweet covered notebook is made from cosy felt, appliquéd with a little woodland deer; perfect for writing down all your thoughts, stories, dreams and big ideas! Felt is such a wonderful craft material, easy to work with and it comes in a rainbow of colours to choose from. Use the templates to sew up your very own Deer Diary and you will find it comes together so quickly that you will want to make up a few more for gifts. Instead of a deer, you might prefer a chicken or a few felt flowers for your cover. Let your imagination run wild!

YOU WILL NEED

Notebook, journal or diary

Tape measure

2 sheets of felt, large enough to cover your chosen notebook

Scraps of multi-coloured felt

Gluestick

Thread

LEVEL

TEMPLATES

Deer scene (see page 137)

INSTRUCTIONS

1. Measuring and cutting the felt

The basic cover consists of 3 rectangle pieces of felt to create the outer cover and the 2 inner flaps that your notebook slips into. First, take some measurements to determine the size of the rectangles you need.

Once you have chosen the notebook you want to cover, use your tape measure to measure around the entire width of your notebook (from the back to the front, including the spine, if any). Add 1cm (³⁄₈in) to this measurement – this will be the whole width of your cover. **(a)**

Now measure the height of your notebook, top to bottom. Add 5mm (¼in) to this measurement – this will be the height of your cover.

You now have the rectangular dimensions (width x height) for the outer cover of your journal that you will cut out from the sheet of felt.

For the inner flaps, subtract 8cm (3in) from the width of the outer cover dimensions and cut out a corresponding rectangle from the second sheet of felt. Cut this piece in half along its height. You now have your two inner flaps that will be sewn on the inside of the outer cover.

Using the templates on page 137, trace or copy the Deer scene. You can re-size them if you like using a photocopier. Cut out the templates and either pin the paper directly to the felt scraps, or trace onto the felt with a fabric marker. **(b)**

When cutting out the felt pieces to be appliquéd onto your cover, I find that using small, sharp embroidery scissors with a fine point at the ends is most beneficial. Cut slowly and carefully around your templates to achieve the best results.

Once you have all of your pieces cut out, it is time to arrange them on your cover.

2. Appliqué the cover

To find the best placement of your appliqué pieces, take your large rectangle cover piece and wrap it loosely around your notebook, situating the overhang evenly. Now arrange that sweet little deer and your scene pieces on the cover until you feel they are just right. **(c)**

You can pin them or use a tiny dab of glue stick to keep them in place, wait a few minutes for the glue to dry before you move on to the stitching. It's now time to appliqué our little buddy to the cover. Using a straight

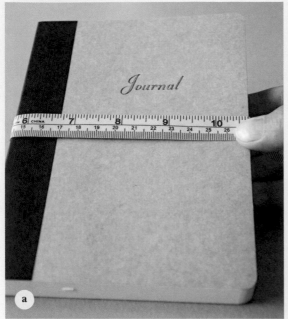

stitch close to the edge of your appliqué piece, begin stitching around your shape, back-stitching at the beginning and end of your stitching to secure the thread. Stitch slowly. With your needle in the down position, lift your presser foot to pivot the cover when you come to a corner or sharp turn in the appliqué piece, and lower the presser foot before continuing to stitch. Repeat this process for all your appliqué pieces. **(d)**

Once you have finished the appliqué on the cover, you can add a label or further embellishment to the inner flap pieces, if you wish.

3. Sew the cover together

Gather up your 3 finished cover pieces. Place each of the inner-flap pieces on opposite ends of the large cover rectangle, wrong sides together and matching raw edges. Pin in place. **(e)**

Firstly, stitch the cover and flaps together all along the top long edge of your cover using a 3mm (⅛in) seam allowance and back-stitching neatly at the beginning and end of your line of stitches. Repeat this process for the long bottom edge.

Now stitch the remaining two side seams with a scant 5mm (¼in) seam allowance, again back-stitching at the start and end of your seam. **(f)**

4. Cover the notebook

To get your notebook all snuggled inside its brand new cover, you will need to open up your notebook and fold back the existing cover on itself. Fold your new felt cover in the same fashion. Gently slide the notebook cover into the inner flaps as shown. **(g)**

If the cover is a little snug, don't fret, as felt will stretch a little after a short time and ease into the perfect fit.

There you have it, all ready to fill with your thoughts and dreams. Happy writing!

TIP

For a nice clean finish at the edges of your notebook cover, use a clear ruler and a rotary cutter to trim a straight line from your seam allowance around the outside edges of your notebook, making sure you don't cut into your stitched seams.

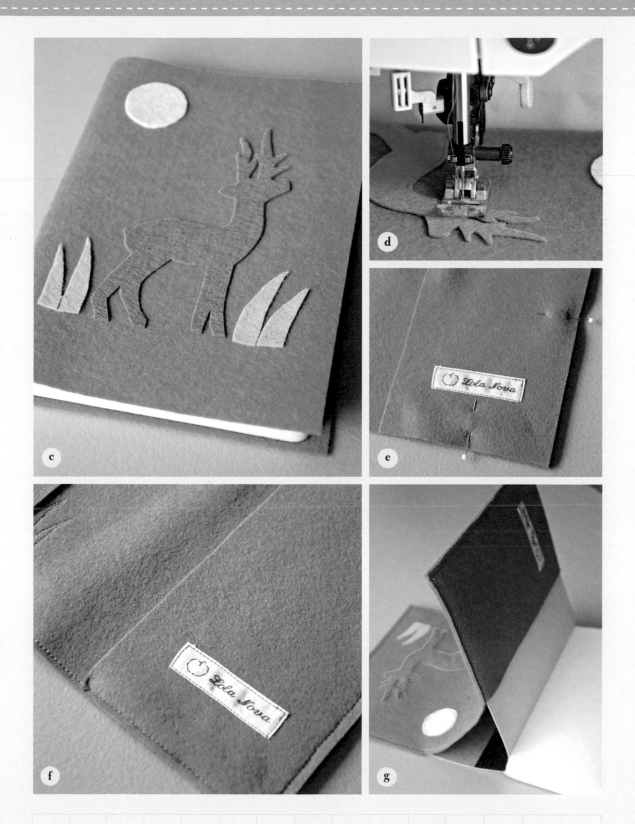

ACTION BELT

Kids are always ready for action, be it the big adventure, the superhero scene, or just everyday life on the go. This Action Belt meets the requirements of any busy kid, with plenty of pockets for carrying an explorer's essentials: a compass, a length of string, and the like. There are also enough pockets for collecting small treasures along the way.

I originally designed this for kids; however once I had made one for my busy kid, I ended up wanting one for myself. It is easy to adjust the waist measurement for a full-grown superhero. I found it perfect for my busy making; I fill the pockets with handy sewing tools and I am always ready for action!

YOU WILL NEED

50 x 114cm (20 x 45in) fabric

50cm (½ yard) light- or medium-weight fusible interfacing

Fabric scraps in different prints

5 buttons or snap fasteners, for pocket closures

Large button, approx. 3–4cm (1¼–1½in) diameter, for belt closure

Thread

 LEVEL

 NOTE

All seam allowances are 1cm (³∕8in) unless otherwise stated

 INSTRUCTIONS

1. Prepare the fabric pieces
For the belt: measure your child's waist, then add 11.5cm (4½in) to this measurement.

Cut 2 strips to the adjusted waist measurement x 8.5cm (3¼in) from the fabric. Cut one strip to the adjusted waist measurement x 8.5cm (3¼in) from the interfacing.

For the pockets: cut four 14.5 x 30cm (5¾ x 11¾in) rectangles from the fabric; two 14.5 x 30cm (5¾ x 11¾in) rectangles from the interfacing; four 11 x 30cm (4¼ x 11¾in) rectangles from the fabric; two 11 x 30cm (4¼ x 11¾in) rectangles from the interfacing. These will make 2 smaller pockets with a lining.

For the loops: cut eight 10.5 x 11cm (4 x 4¼in) rectangles from the fabric. **(a)**

Fuse the corresponding interfacing pieces to the lining pieces of the belt and pockets, following the manufacturer's instructions.

2. Make the belt
Pin together the exterior and lining pieces of the belt strips with right sides facing and raw edges matching.

Stitch around 3 sides, leaving one short end open. Clip the corners. **(b)**

Turn the belt right side out, fold under the seam allowance on the open end, and press. Top-stitch around all edges; this will close the opening. **(c)**

3. Make the pocket loops
Fold the rectangles in half lengthways with wrong sides facing, and press to create a centre crease. Open the loop piece and turn in each raw edge to meet at the centre crease. Press. Fold in half again and press. **(d)**

Top-stitch along all the edges, then fold under 1cm (³∕8in) at each end, press and set aside. **(e)**

4. Make the pockets
Pin the exterior and lining pieces together with right sides facing and raw edges matching. Stitch around all edges leaving a 7.5cm (3in) opening along one short edge for turning.

Turn right side out, folding under the seam allowance at the opening and press. Top-stitch along the short edge to close the opening.

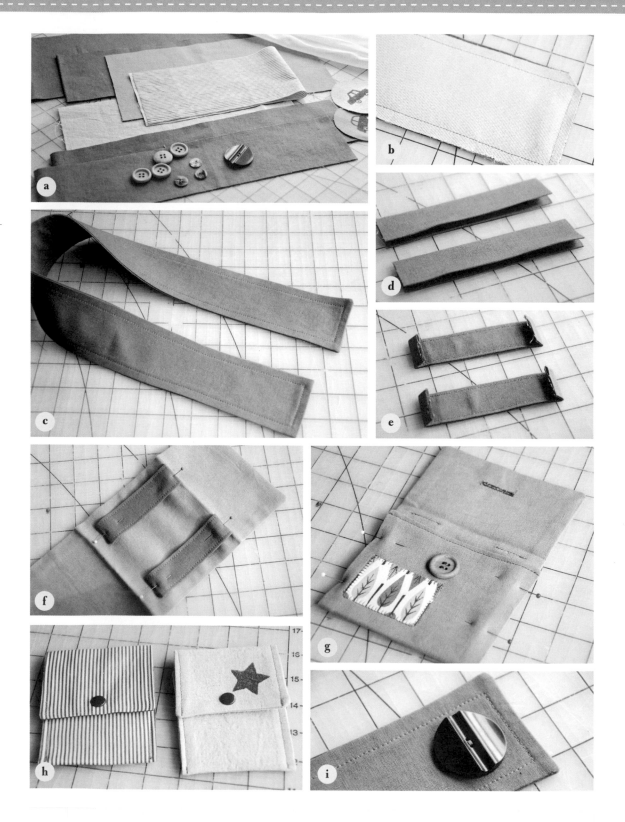

Fold the pocket at 6cm (2⅜in) from one end (the top) and at 9.5cm (3¾in) from the other end, creating a "billfold". Press.

Pin the loops onto the exterior of the pocket 1.5cm (⅝in) from the sides and 6cm (2⅜in) from the top edge (or along the crease). Stitch in place close to the folded edge of the loops on either end. **(f)**

Add a little embellishment to the pocket now if you like. Sew a buttonhole in the top fold of the pocket (see page 20). Using your folds as guides, mark the placement of the button on the outside bottom fold and sew on your button. Pin the bottom fold of the pocket as shown. **(g)**

Stitch together along the sides, close to the edge. Top-stitch around the edges of the pocket flap.

Repeat this process to make up the remaining pockets. Using snap fasteners instead of buttons for your pocket closures is a nice option. **(h)**

5. Finish the belt

Fit the belt around your child's waist to find the best placement for a buttonhole and button and mark. Sew a buttonhole and button on the ends of the belt (see page 20). **(i)**

Slide the pockets onto the belt through the loops.

Put the belt on a busy kid and…ready, set, go!

TIP

Make extra pockets in different fabrics for interchangeable action. An Action Belt made out of heavy-duty canvas with larger pockets would be perfect for a handyman, fisherman or superman!

It is so simple to make your own sew-on patches and badges for embellishing just about everything. This is a truly whimsical project; perfect for using up those itty bitty treasured scraps, and for using your imagination. I am going to show you a few techniques and examples of what you can do, but by no means are these the limit of what you can create.

I have made these for kids' clothing, of course, as well as my own clothing, backpacks, bags, luggage, jackets... and the list goes on and on. You can use many of the techniques in this book for making patches and badges, too.

YOU WILL NEED

Fabric scraps

Felt scraps

Fusible interfacing

Fabric marker or pencil

Thread

Bias binding tape

Trims, ribbons, ricrac, buttons and so on

LEVEL

NOTE

There are no precise instructions for this project; rather I'll be showing you techniques and ideas to help you on your way.

 INSTRUCTIONS

1. Make a small round patch

First, gather some happy scraps of fabric and felt; when you have chosen one to start with, attach a piece of fusible interfacing to the wrong side of your fabric. **(a)**

To make a round patch, use a glass or other round object to mark a circle on your fabric with a fabric marker. Do the same on a scrap of felt for the backing. **(b) (c)**

Pin the fabric circle onto the felt circle evenly. Attach some bias-binding tape to the outer edge of the circle, pinning in place as you go. Fold under the end of your bias binding and pin. **(d)**

Stitch the bias binding in place. I have found that using a zigzag stitch to attach the bias binding for small round patches works well. Your patch is now ready to be sewn on! You can use a hand-stitch method or your machine to attach the patch.

2. Make a large round patch

A similar technique is used for the large round badge. I have used two different fabrics with fusible interfacing

already attached, so there is no need for a felt backing. Cut one circle from the featured fabric. Cut a larger circle from the background fabric. **(e)**

Centre the smaller circle on top of the larger circle and pin in place. I have chosen some ricrac to go around the outer edge of the centre circle. **(f)**

Stitch the ricrac so that it overlaps the edge of the centre circle all the way around. Again, I have found that a zigzag stitch accomplishes this quite nicely. **(g)**

The last step is to attach bias binding to the outer edge of the large circle.

The patch is now ready to embellish anything and everything – pockets on jeans, a school backpack, an apron...

3. More ideas

This example uses the ricrac on the outer edge of the patch. The centre circle is attached using a blanket stitch on my machine; a zigzag or satin machine stitch would also be suitable. **(h)**

A small round patch

a

b

c

d

A large round patch

e

f

g

More ideas

h

i

Another idea

j

Add a loop of ribbon to the bottom of the badge, attached to the back. After you have sewn your patch to its new home, add a button for interest. **(i)**

4. Another idea

Use rubber stamps and fabric paint to create a badge (see page 12). Apply the motif, let it dry and set according to the manufacturer's instructions.

Next cut the motif out and attach it to a background piece of fabric (I've used felt here) using your preferred method. Finish with a few embellishments, such as buttons and ricrac. **(j)**

As you can see, just a few tools and some imagination is all it takes to create a treasure trove of cool patches and badges. Now go!

In our modern age, the art of the handwritten note seems to be all but disappearing. Imagine receiving a beautiful, one-of-a-kind, handcrafted stitched note card in the post. How wonderful!

This is the perfect rainy day scrappy project. If you have never stitched on paper, this is a great introduction, as well as a wonderfully creative way to use up those itty bitty scraps you can't bear to part with. This is a casual how-to: let imagination and whimsy be your guide. There truly is no limit to what you can create – make a set of six and give them as a special gift!

YOU WILL NEED

One sheet of A4 (letter size/11¾ x 8½in) cardstock in colour of choice for each card

One C5 229 x 192mm (A9/5¾ x 8¾in) envelope for each card

Scraps of felt, fabric and trims in various sizes

Small buttons

Fabric glue

Large sheet of felt and fabric scraps for envelope (optional)

LEVEL

INSTRUCTIONS

1. Cottage note card

Begin by folding a sheet of cardstock in half widthways. Choose some scraps in a colour scheme that pleases you. For this first example, I'll show you how to make a little cottage note card using 3 rectangles and one triangle.

For the body of the house I like to use a plain colour of felt. Cut a rectangle approx. 7.5 x 10cm (3 x 4in). Then cut a smaller rectangle out of a complementary fabric approx. 2.5 x 5cm (1 x 2in) for a door. Cut one triangle sized proportionately for the roof and, finally, cut a wee rectangle for a chimney.

Lay out your cut pieces on top of the folded cardstock, moving them around until you have the look just right. **(a)**

Starting with the larger felt rectangle, put just a spot of glue in the centre back to keep it in place on the card. I set my machine to a slightly longer stitch than I use for normal sewing and use a medium-gauge needle.

Stitch the felt rectangle directly to the cardstock close to the edge of the felt with a contrasting colour thread, back-stitch one or two stitches at the beginning and end of your stitching and trim your threads. **(b)**

Add the rest of your elements to the card, stitching them one at a time. You can use a simple decorative stitch, if

you desire, but stay away from heavy embroidery-type machine stitches, as they can rip your cardstock.

Add a small button as a doorknob or design element. **(c)** Make a whole set of cards in houses of different colours!

2. Fashion note card

Now for a little fashion design! Possibilities are endless here, so I am simply going to show you how to make a pretty skirt for a fashion-inspired note card.

Start with a rectangle, approx. 10 x 12.5cm (4 x 5in), turn under and press all of the raw edges by approx. 5mm (¼in).

Using the longest stitch on your machine, or a gathering stitch, stitch along one long edge of the rectangle, do not back-stitch and do not trim threads. Pull on the threads to gather the top of the rectangle. **(d)**

Stitch the skirt directly to the card front along the two short sides, as shown. **(e)**

You can now cut out a little felt jumper to go with your skirt or, as I did, just cut out a simple little tank-top shape and tuck it into the top of the skirt. Stitch it down to the card.

To pull the outfit all together, simply tie a bow in some narrow ribbon and stitch to the card. **(f)**

Cottage note card

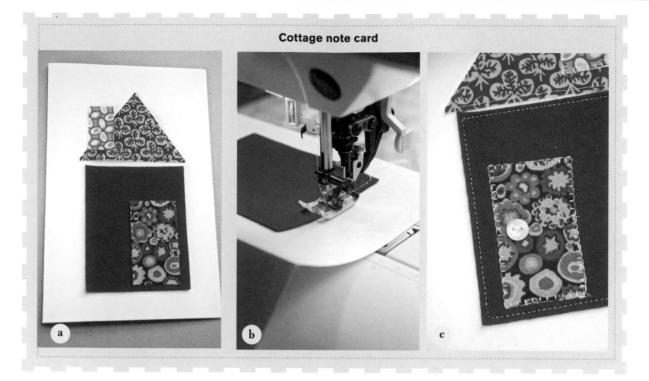

a

b

c

Now, write your note, slip the card into an envelope and mail it to someone special.

3. Gift envelope

Cut a large sheet of felt into a 26 x 45cm (10¼ x 17¾in) rectangle. Decorate the rectangle in any way you like; sew on ribbon, patchwork, etc.

Fold up 18.5cm (7¼in) of one short edge of the rectangle, pin in place along both sides creating an envelope, as shown. **(g)**

Stitch along the pinned sides using a 5mm (¼in) seam allowance; do not sew the top flap in your seams. Fold over the top flap of the envelope and press. **(h)**

Use the envelope to keep your Stitched Note Cards protected or as the perfect gift wrapping for a set of handmade cards.

TIP

Due to the added weight of the cards, it would be wise to check on the postage before mailing.

WHIMSY

Fashion note card

d

e

f

Gift envelope

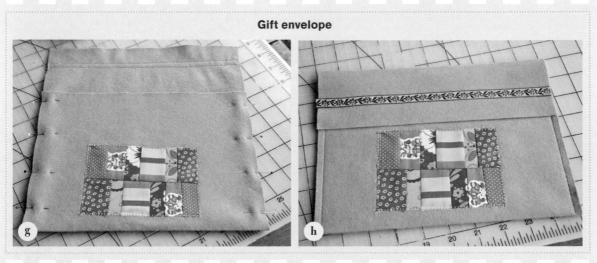

g

h

WEE BUNNY

"Once upon a time, there was a wee bunny named Mow, pronounced "Mo" with a long "o" sound. He made his home in a cosy den at the foot of an impressive elderberry bush, which was part of the overgrown garden that belonged to the Little Green Cottage. He was quite content and felt most fortunate that the inhabitants of the Little Green Cottage not only had a most impressive elderberry bush, but that they had also put in a rather satisfactory vegetable garden. The only downside to his nearly idyllic situation was that he had to share the garden with an unfortunate number of neighbourhood cats. Still, it was looking to be a swell year; Mow had noticed that a lovely patch of Savoy cabbage was just about ready for nibbling. He had grand plans to invite all of his Wee Bunny friends over for a feast, but that, my dears, is a story for another time."

Wee Bunny came to life while I was remembering some of my own beloved childhood soft toys –toys handmade for me by a family friend; the best kind! Wee Bunny is the perfect size and shape for little hands to hold on to. Whether made from felt, or a special piece of cherished fabric, each bunny is simply and wonderfully loveable.

YOU WILL NEED

One 33 x 33cm (13 x 13in) square of coloured felt, or fabric of choice, for the body and ears of the bunny

One 15 x 15cm (6 x 6in) square of white or cream felt, for the face and tail

One 15 x 15cm (6 x 6in) square of complementary fabric, for the ear linings

Freezer paper

Thread

Small embroidery hoop (optional)

Black embroidery thread (or colour of choice) and embroidery needle

Polyester, cotton or wool toy stuffing (the amount of stuffing you will need depends on which stuffing you use. I used approximately 25g/1oz of polyester fibrefill)

Long pencil or chopstick

LEVEL

TEMPLATES

Bunny face, Bunny ears, Bunny body, Bunny tail (see page 137)

INSTRUCTIONS

1. Prepare the fabric pieces

Copy or trace the templates from page 137 onto freezer-paper to make your pattern. Cut out the paper pattern pieces. Fold the large square of felt or fabric in half, pin the body and ear pattern pieces to both layers of the felt or fabric, and cut out. You should have 2 body pieces and 2 ear pieces. **(a)**

Cut out 1 bunny tail shape from white or cream coloured felt. Fold the square of ear lining fabric in half, pin the ear pattern piece through both layers of fabric, and cut out. You should have 2 ear lining pieces.

2. Embroider the bunny's face

Trace the circle face template onto the square of white or cream felt using a fabric marker or pencil; transfer the face of the bunny onto the felt in the same manner.

Centre your markings inside a small embroidery hoop; you may alternatively embroider your felt without a hoop as felt has a bit of body to it, making it easy to work with.

Thread your embroidery needle with the embroidery thread and embroider the bunny's face onto the felt, using straight stitch and back stitch (see page 21). **(b)**

Following your markings, cut out the circle of felt for the bunny's face, then cut out the bunny's tail from the remainder, using the template as a guide.

3. Sew the bunny's ears

Pin an ear lining to each of the felt or main fabric pieces, right sides together, and stitch around the two long edges using a 3mm (1/8in) seam allowance, leaving the base of the ear open for turning.

Turn the ears right side out and press. Fold the ears in half with the felt or main fabric on the outside and pin in place. **(c)**

Starting at the folded edge, close to the raw edges of the base of the ear, sew a few stitches – about half of the folded width of the ear, then back-stitch. This creates the little pleat in the ear.

4. Assemble the bunny's body

Pin the bunny's face to the right side of one of the body pieces. Centre the face about 2cm (3/4in) from the top of the body piece. **(d)**

Pin the bunny's tail to the right side of the other body piece. Centre the tail about 3cm (1 1/4in) from the bottom of the body piece, as shown. **(e)**

Stitch both the face and the tail to the body pieces; sew close to the edge using either a straight stitch or a simple decorative stitch, such as a zigzag stitch. I used a stitch that mimics a blanket stitch (see Glossary, page 140) for Mow's face. **(f)**

Take the body piece with the face attached and mark a small dot at the centre of the top of the head. Place an ear, with lining side facing the right side of the bunny, about 1–1.5cm (3/8–5/8in) to one side of the centre dot and pin in place. Repeat with the remaining ear on the other side of the centre dot. Point the tips of the ears slightly inward and overlapping as shown. **(g)**

Tack the ears in place close to the raw edges.

Take the body piece with the tail attached to it and place it on top of the body piece with the ears and face, with the right sides together and the raw edges matching. Pin around the outer edges and stitch the body using a 5mm (1/4in) seam allowance, making sure to leave the bottom open for turning.

Reach inside the sewn bunny and grab the tips of the ears with your fingers; pull the ears gently to turn the bunny right side out.

5. Fill the bunny with stuffing

Start filling your bunny with stuffing, half handfuls at a time. Pull the stuffing into small pieces before you insert it. I used a long pencil or chopstick to help push the stuffing up into the head. For the best effect, stuff the bunny as tightly and as full as you can. **(h)**

Once your bunny is stuffed, it is time to close the opening by hand. Thread a needle with a double length of thread and make a knot at the end. Turn under the seam allowance at the opening and begin stitching the opening closed using slip stitch, making sure to pull your stitches tight as you go. When you are finished, cut the thread leaving a short length to tie off with a knot, then trim the threads. **(i)**

Now you have an adorable Wee Bunny of your own, make him some friends and let the adventures begin!

Fox (page 63)

Hare (page 63)

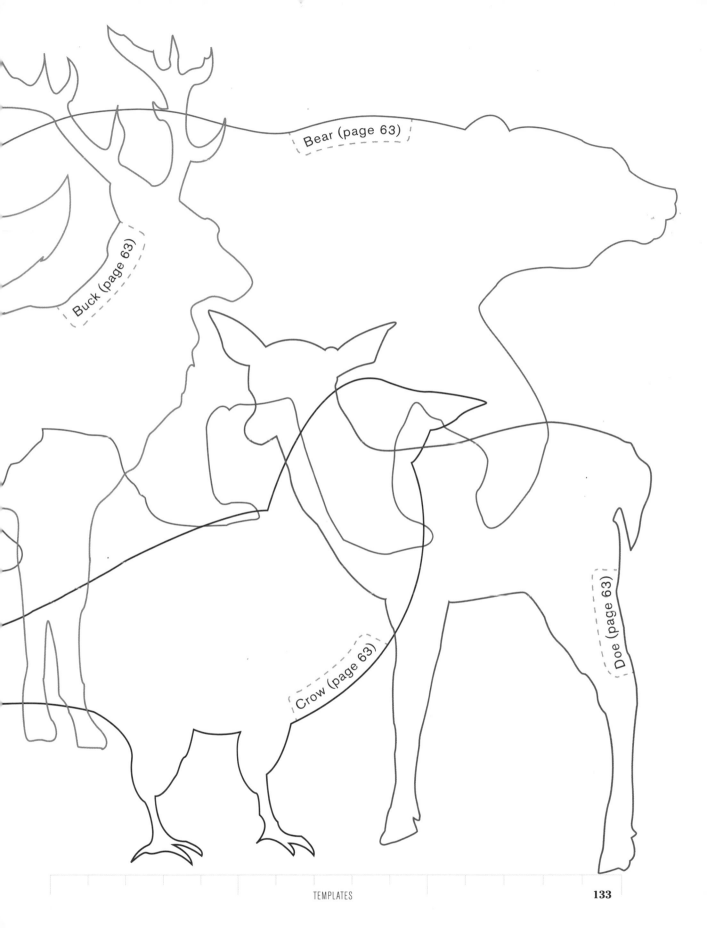

Bear (page 63)

Buck (page 63)

Doe (page 63)

Crow (page 63)

Eagle (page 63)

Owl (page 63)

Wolf (page 63)

TEMPLATES

Squirrel (page 63)

Stag head (page 63)

Fir trees (page 63)

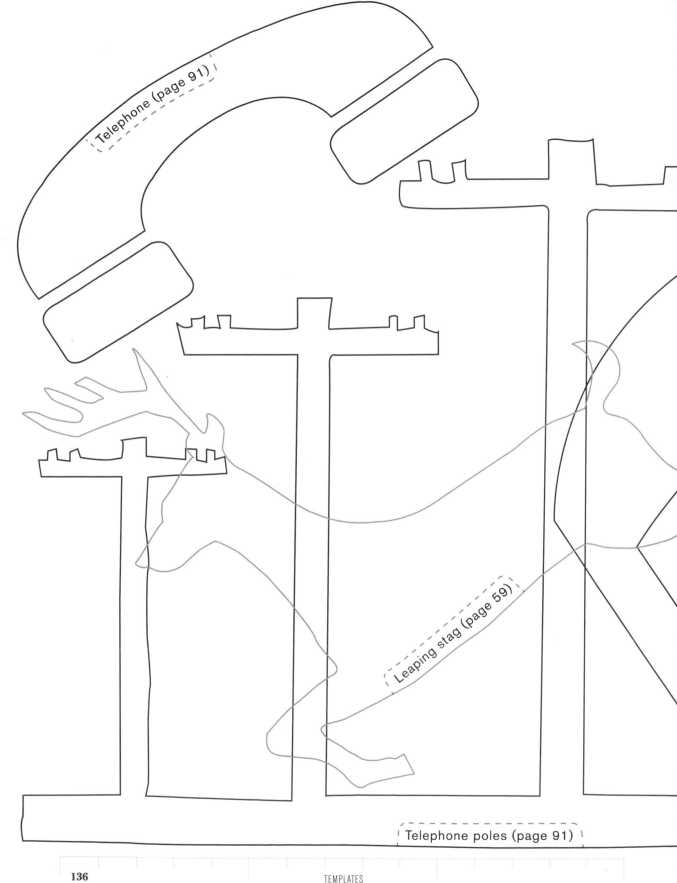

Telephone (page 91)

Leaping stag (page 59)

Telephone poles (page 91)

Bunny face (page 129)

Bunny body (page 129)

Bunny ears (page 129)

Bunny tail (page 129)

Deer scene (page 113)

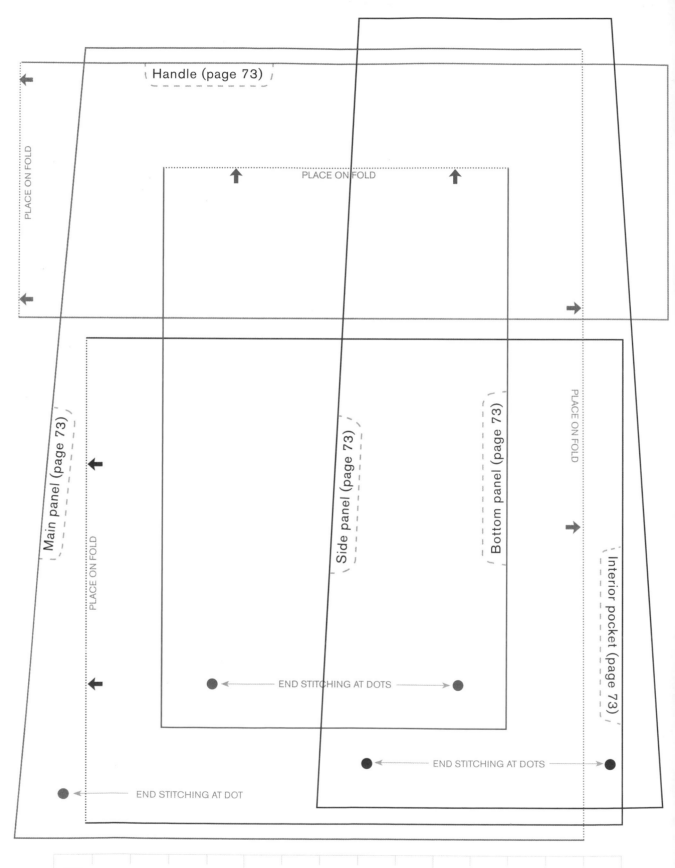

Handle (page 73)

PLACE ON FOLD

PLACE ON FOLD

Main panel (page 73)

PLACE ON FOLD

Side panel (page 73)

Bottom panel (page 73)

PLACE ON FOLD

Interior pocket (page 73)

END STITCHING AT DOTS

END STITCHING AT DOTS

END STITCHING AT DOT

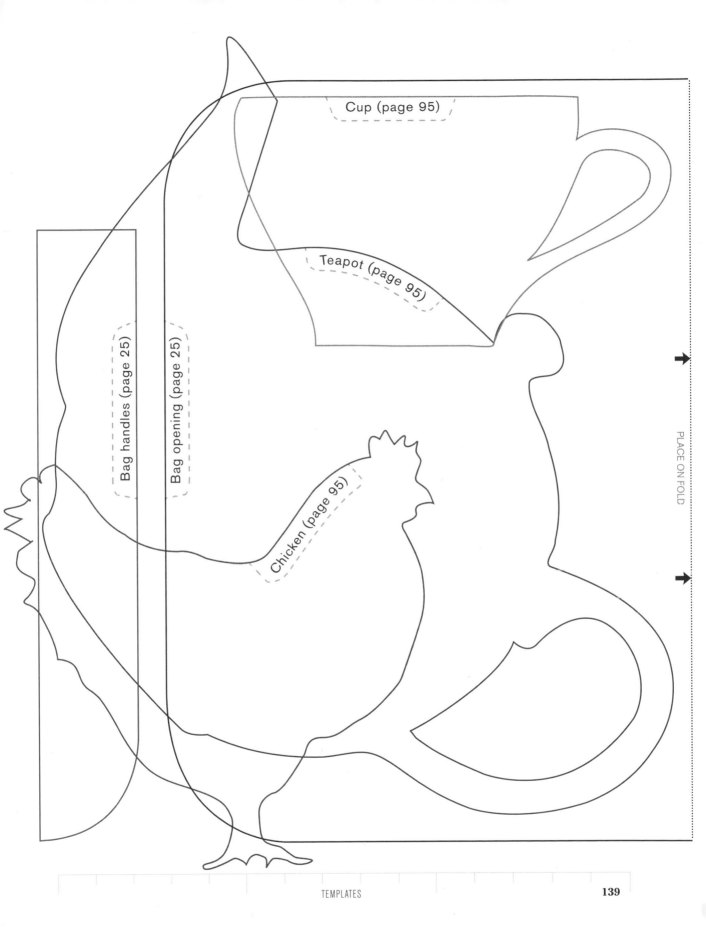

Cup (page 95)

Teapot (page 95)

Bag handles (page 25)

Bag opening (page 25)

Chicken (page 95)

PLACE ON FOLD

GLOSSARY

Back stitch Also known as back tacking, a stitch used at the beginning and end of a machine-sewn seam to anchor the seam in place; it involves a couple of extra stitches back and forth. Also a hand-embroidery stitch used for outlining.

Bias A line marked at a 45-degree angle across the fabric, used for cutting bias-binding strips or to cut fabric on the bias.

Bias binding/Tape Strips of fabric cut on the bias, often turned under and pressed, and used for bindings, facings or other applications where there is a need for stretch or accommodation to curves. Often found finishing the edge of a blanket or quilt.

Blanket stitch A hand stitch often worked along the edge of fabric or to appliqué fabric pieces. Some sewing machines have a decorative blanket-stitch option.

Bodice The upper body piece of a garment.

Bodkin A blunt-ended needle that is used for threading elastic through casings in waists or cuffs on garments.

Casing A channel created in a piece of fabric between two rows of stitching through which is threaded cord or elastic to create a drawstring or gathered waist.

Directional fabrics Fabrics bearing a design that has a clear direction (one way is up).

Double hem A double hem encloses the raw edge and makes a durable basic hem suitable for children's clothes, aprons and simple garments. A double hem works well on trousers and any tops with straight hems. This hem can be very narrow and so suitable for curved hems, or quite deep, which is best used on straight hems only.

Ease/Easing A way of sewing a length of fabric into a smaller space without resulting in gathers or puckers. Also, a seam or other addition that allows a garment to fit the body better.

Facing This is usually a separate piece of fabric attached to the inside of a garment to finish raw edges, such as on a neckline or armhole. Occasionally the facing is an extension of the main fabric.

Grain This refers to the direction of the threads in a piece of fabric, either running lengthways or crossways.

Hem/Hemline The fabric that is turned up on the lower edge of a garment, sleeve or raw edge of a sewing project to provide a finished edge. Hemline can refer to the length of garment, or the area of the hem.

Interfacing A material (available in a variety of weights/thicknesses/flexibility) used between layers of fabric to provide stabilization and form. It is available in a fusible or sewn-in form.

Lining Used to finish the inside of a garment, or other sewn item such as bags, purses and pouches, to hide the seam construction, and to provide decorative effect. A lining is cut from the same pattern pieces as the sewn item.

Muslin A generally inexpensive woven fabric used to make crafts, back quilts or to make draft or test garments.

Placket The piece of fabric that reinforces a split or opening in a garment. Usually also serves as the closure.

Right side The right side of the fabric is the design side or the outer or visible side. There are instances of fabric with no right or wrong side visible, and the determination and appropriate markings are then made by the person doing the pattern cutting and sewing.

Seam A stitched line formed where two pieces of material are stitched together along their margins or preset line.

Seam allowance The amount of fabric between the edge of the fabric and the line of stitching or seam.

Selvedge The selvedge refers to the edge of fabric as it comes off the bolt. The selvedge is the edges of the fabric which has manufacturer information. This area of the fabric is usually a bound edge that does not fray. It should not be included when you cut your fabric as it can cause puckering or distortion.

Slip stitch A small, almost invisible, hand stitch, sometimes called ladder stitch, used to secure small gaps or openings in hems or seams. It is worked through the fold on both sides, catching a thread on the opposite side to make a stitch.

Stencil A template made by cutting a design into paper, plastic, cardboard or metal. Also, a method of applying a design by brushing ink or paint through the cut-out areas of a template so that the pattern will be reproduced on the surface below.

Stitch in the ditch Sewing on top of a finished seamline from the front of the garment. The stitch goes through all layers and holds them together.

Straight stitch A standard machine stitch used for most general sewing purposes, available in different stitch lengths to suit the fabric.

Tack/Tacking A temporary method of holding two or more layers of fabric together by sewing by hand or machine with long stitches, usually removed after final stitching.

Top stitch Visible, decorative stitching done on the outside of the garment or project close to a seam or edge; also called accent stitching.

Wrong side The wrong side of the fabric is the reverse side upon which there is no decorative design, such as a print, or the inside of an item.

Zigzag stitch A machine stitch that is used to finish seam edges or as a decorative stitch to appliqué two pieces together.

RESOURCES

Brick and Mortar Shops

New Fabric & Haberdashery (UK)

Bedecked
5 Castle Street
Hay-on-Wye
Hereford HR3 5DF
+44 (0)1497 822769
www.bedecked.co.uk

Cloth House
47 Berwick Street
London W1F 8SJ
+44 (0)20 7437 5155
www.clothhouse.com

Fabrics Galore
52–54 Lavender Hill
London SW11 5RH
+44 (0)20 7738 9589
www.fabricsgalore.co.uk

Fabric Rehab
3b Dedham Vale Business Centre
Manningtree Road, Dedham
Essex CO7 6BL
+44 (0)1206 321611
www.fabricrehab.co.uk

John Lewis
Oxford Street
London W1A 1EX
and stores nationwide
08456 049049 (from the UK)
+44 (0)1698 545454
www.johnlewis.com

Liberty
Regent Street
London W1B 5AH
+44 (0)20 7734 1234
www.liberty.co.uk

MacCulloch & Wallis
25–26 Dering Street
London W1S 1AT
+44 (0)20 7629 0311
www.macculloch-wallis.co.uk

Millie Moon Haberdashery Boutique
24–25 Catherine Hill
Frome
Somerset BA11 1BY
+44 (0)1373 464650
www.milliemoonshop.co.uk

Ray Stitch Haberdashery Shop
99 Essex Road
London N1 2SJ
+44 (0)20 7704 1060
www.raystitch.co.uk

New Fabric & Haberdashery (US & Australia)

Bolt Fabric Boutique
2136 NE Alberta St
Portland, OR 97211
USA
503.287.bolt
www.boltfabricboutique.com

Britex Fabrics
146 Geary St
San Francisco, CA 94108
USA
(415) 392.2910
www.britexfabrics.com

Purl Soho
459 Broome St
New York, NY 10013
USA
(800) 597.7875
www.purlsoho.com/purl

Patchwork on Central Park
148 Burke Rd
East Malvern VIC 3145
AUSTRALIA
61 3 9885 4480
www.patchworkoncentralpark.com.au

Online Shops

New Fabric & Haberdashery

www.backstitch.co.uk
www.banberryplace.com
www.craftymamas.com.au
www.duckcloth.com.au
www.kleins.co.uk
www.pinkchalkfabrics.com
www.sewmamasew.com
www.sewmehappy.co.uk
www.thefabricloft.co.uk

Vintage Fabrics

www.donnaflower.com
www.etsy.com
www.ebay.com
www.materialpleasures.com
www.revivalfabrics.com
www.spinstersemporium.com
www.vintagefabrics.com.au

Fabric Paint & Materials

www.craftyarts.co.uk
www.dharmatrading.com
http://direct.hobbycraft.co.uk
www.fabricandart.com
www.rainbowsilks.co.uk

Felt

http://stores.americanfeltandcraft.com
www.bloomingfelt.co.uk

INDEX

M

marking tools 8
measurements 16
measuring tools 8

N

Natural 45
    Elemental Fabric Canvas 50–3
    Gathering Bag 54–7
    Into the Woods Throw 62–5,
        132–5
    Pockets Full of Posies 46–9
    Stag Cushion Cover 58–61, 136
needles 8
Note Cards 124–7
notebooks 9

O

organizers 9
    Urban Organizer 106–9

P

paper patterns 9
Patches 120–3
pattern-making 16
    creating pattern from existing
        garment 17–18
    modifying existing pattern 18–19
    taking key measurements 16
pencils 8
pens 8
pincushions 8
pinking shears 9, 21
pins 8
Pockets Full of Posies 46–9
pressing 21

R

ribbons 11
ricrac 11

rotary cutters 9
rubber stamps 9, 12
rulers 8, 9
running stitch 21

S

safety pins 8
satin stitch 21
scissors 8
seam gauges 9
seam rippers 8
seams, finishing 21
sewing machines 8
    needles 8
shirts
    Gypsy Shirt and Jacket 28–33
skirts
    Skipping Skirt 40–3
Stag Cushion Cover 58–61
    templates 136
stencils
    freezer paper stencils 13
Stitched Note Cards 124–7
straight pins 8
Summer Tent 34–7

T

tape measures 8
Tea Towel of Distinction 94–7
    templates 139
templates
    "Call Me" Cushion Cover 136
    Deer Diary 137
    Into the Woods Throw 132–5
    Lola Handbag 138
    Stag Cushion Cover 136
    Tea Towel of Distinction 139
    Vagabond Bag 139
    Wee Bunny 137
thread 8

throws
    Into the Woods Throw 62–5,
        132–5
toys
    Wee Bunny 128–31, 137
trims 11

U

Urban Organizer 106–9

V

Vagabond Bag 24–7
    templates 139
Vintage 67
    Hook Book 76–9
    In Dreams Fabric Headboard
        84–7
    Little Joy Dress 68–71
    Lola Handbag 72–5, 138
    Vintage Laundry Bag 80–3
vintage fabrics 11

W

Wee Bunny 128–31
    templates 137
Whimsy 111
    Action Belt 116–19
    Badges and Patches 120–3
    Deer Diary 112–15, 137
    Stitched Note Cards 124–7
    Wee Bunny 128–31, 137

Z

zips 21

INDEX   143

ACKNOWLEDGEMENTS

Many thanks are owed to the wonderful people without whom this book would not be possible. Huge thanks go to Alison Starling and her colleagues at Octopus Publishing Group, for having faith in me and providing me with this amazing opportunity. To my editor, Katie Hardwicke, thank you for your keen eye and patience, such a joy to work with. Much gratitude goes to Yuki Sugiura for the lovely photographs.

Very special thanks to my wonderfully supportive husband, Andrew, who encouraged me and cheered me on. He also doubled as proofreader, math wizard, morale booster, chief cook and bottle washer; I could not have done this without you. Thank you my love.

Special thanks to some very special people – Tif Fussell, Nancy Langdon and Jane Grimshaw; I am so grateful for the kindness, advice, wisdom, time and support that you gave to me. Thanks to my mother Susan, for the encouragement, the beautiful vintage fabrics and for giving me her 1979 Bernina 830 sewing machine all those years ago. Thank you my sweet daughter Stella, for the endless inspiration and everyday joy.

Finally, a very special thank you to the readers and friends of my blog *Lola Nova – Whatever Lola Wants*, who inspire me every day: without you, this book would not have been possible.
http://lolanovablog.blogspot.com

The publisher would like to thank Virginia Armstrong of fabric and wallpaper company Roddy & Ginger for providing a wonderful location for our photography.
www.roddyandginger.co.uk